Came to Believe

A Journey of Trust, Faith and Perseverance

Tara Danielle LaDue

For the generations of LaDue women who give me strength:

My Grandma, Edith,
My Mother, Judee,
and My Beautiful Niece

"Once you believe in yourself and see your soul as divine and precious, you will automatically become a being who can create a miracle."
-Dr. Wayne Dyer

Contents

Chapter One
Where It All Began

"Patience and perseverance have a magical effect
before which difficulties disappear
and obstacles vanish."
-John Quincy Adams

When I was in school, I loved to write.
Writing short stories, which allowed me an outlet to
fantasize and escape, saved me. I had the freedom of
expression in my storytelling, and I could say
anything that I wanted to without having to worry
about who I would hurt or how it would make others
feel. Often, I wrote about things that were true for
me, but I made my teacher believe that it was fiction.
I usually wrote in two spectrums, comedy or drama;
something funny that got my classmates attention
when I read it out loud or on another very dark topic
that alarmed my teachers. I've written in journals
since the 7th grade, first at the assignment of my
teachers, then it turned into much more. It was an
outcry for attention. It was my therapy. I started a
book in my 20's about my life and childhood. Back
then I wasn't a believer in the power of
manifestation, and I didn't have any idea of a Higher
Power. I didn't even know what manifestation was. I
didn't believe in myself. I didn't think my story

mattered. Who cares? I couldn't be an author because my book would never get published. A lot of "I didn't, I couldn't and never." I was so young then and thought I had a lot to say, but who would listen? My first unpublished book was a tale of victimhood. It was a way to hold on to the past and not move forward. That book was keeping me in my ego and didn't have great intentions. No wonder it never materialized. This is a much different book. I promise.

I grew up in a single-parent home and was raised by my mother. I had four other siblings, three of the oldest ones and I lived with my mom. I have an older adopted brother and sister and an older biological brother. My mom was just 29 years old when she became a single mother of four little children. I never lived in a home with a father and had no idea what it was like to have a positive male figure in my life. My dad left, and my parents divorced before I was born. He remarried after the divorce. I did see my father twice a week, but it wasn't enough. It was a complicated relationship, and I often felt in the middle between my mom and dad, not wanting to hurt their feelings, specifically my mom's feelings. I acted in the perfect way and said the right things to not rock the boat. That is a lot of responsibility to put on kid's shoulders and it taught me that I could not say what I felt or have any feelings at all because it would make others unhappy.

I liked going to my dad's house. But, I couldn't show it. When we visited him, everything seemed like a normal family there. We would have lunch and dinner at the table together. We always had a tall glass of milk with each meal that we could mix in Hershey's chocolate syrup or Strawberry Quick. What kid wouldn't love that? After dinner, if we ate our food, excused ourselves properly and asked politely, we could have a piece of Bubble Yum gum. After lunch and dinner, we played in the front yard or went swimming with all the neighborhood kids. It was nice. It felt safe. I do remember, however, was always getting headaches at my dad's house and having to lie down with one of those red rubber things filled with hot water, while my dad would play the Eagles on his guitar. Now, I realize that those headaches stemmed from the anxiety of going back home to my house where my mom's feelings would be hurt if I said I had fun at my dad's.

I have been deeply affected by the disease of alcoholism. My mother is a recovering alcoholic with over 11 years of sobriety. I am extremely proud of her. It's not easy to remain sober and it requires daily perseverance. My mother got sober when I was

30, and I am so grateful that this finally happened. I prayed and begged God to make her stop drinking for years. I did everything I could to get her sober. I am now in my forties. From as long as I can remember my mother drank during most of my childhood. I don't have many memories from the age five and younger. I would say I didn't learn a whole lot about relationships, and what I did learn wasn't a very loving example. Now, when I think about my mother being thirty years old, divorced and a single mom with four children, I cry. Tears are welling in my eyes right now. I try to put myself in her shoes, and I cannot do it. What was she feeling? When I was thirty my mom was just getting sober; my older biological brother was serving in Iraq, I lived in Los Angeles and worked in fashion at a job I hated. I took care of no one but myself. I had to feed and dress no one but myself. My time was my time. I didn't have to get anyone to school, do homework, go to the grocery store with four kids to manage. My mom was alone and depressed. Being forty now, I still can't imagine my life as a single mother of four children. I can have compassion for my mother now, but growing up I didn't understand her disease.

My mom did the best she could. I know she loved us, but it was rough for her which made it

rough for us kids. With me being sensitive and an
empath, I was hugely affected by what was going on,
or not going on, in my home. My mom was my
temperature check. If she was happy, I was happy. If
she was sad, I was sad. She didn't have the best of
jobs or a college education, but she always made sure
we had what we wanted as far as the popular brands
of clothes and participating in whatever extra-
curricular activities we chose, even if it meant putting
it on a credit card or layaway. She used to take me to
Mervyn's or Miller's Outpost to buy a new outfit to
wear on my birthday at school. Even though we
always shopped the clearance racks, we made it
happen. I was fortunate enough to play the alto
saxophone in school, play softball and to be in Girl
Scouts. I am grateful to my mom for never losing
sight through her alcoholism of how important it was
for children to explore creatively and be involved in
activities.

Throughout my early years, there were a lot of
unfortunate experiences. I didn't grow up in a stable
home. I learned very early to do what made my mom
happy and tried not to upset her or challenge her
because that might make her drink more. I was my
mom's biggest supporter and confidant, two things I
shouldn't have had to worry about as a child. My
mom worked hard. She worked full time while

raising my brothers and sister, trying to juggle all of our activities and paying the bills at the same time. My dad did pay child support every week, but it never seemed enough. I remember them going to court several times fighting about child support with us kids being in the middle. There wasn't money to pay for music camps, Catalina trips or softball. There was even a time when we didn't have health insurance or dental care. We got free lunches at school and free dental check ups through our school district.

My Grandma Edith would always step in to help out for those kinds of things. I am truly grateful for her, and I loved my grandma very much. She was extremely strong, independent and always stepped in for us kids when my mom wasn't able to. I lived with my grandma for two years while I finished college. I felt quite lucky to have that time with her before she succumbed to Alzheimer's. She saved the day a lot while I was growing up. When my mom's car broke down, she would pay to fix it. When my mom was short in paying the mortgage, my grandma would help out. Several times our air conditioner broke, in Phoenix, Arizona's 120-degree temperatures, and my grandma stepped in to fix it time and time again, either paying to repair the AC or replace it. We slept in the living room with wet towels, frozen liter bottles of water and fans during those times. It was hot, sweaty, embarrassing and truly awful. Because of things always breaking down and needing to be fixed, it caused me a lot of anxiety around owning a car or house. I was taught to think the worst-case scenario, so I would be prepared to deal with anything. Even though living with that kind of negative thinking is not the path that I would have chosen, I am at my best when the shit hits the fan. I am very resourceful and a survivor. Luckily today I have a posse of angels by my side and have learned that I no longer have to rely solely on my own strength. I love the quote from *A Course in Miracles*, "If you knew who walks beside you on the path that you have chosen, fear would be impossible."

I am also a survivor of childhood sexual abuse. To type that very sentence right now paralyzes me. I stared at my computer screen for a few minutes with my eyes glazed over and tears welling. Now as I am writing this chapter, the thought of including a chapter in this book about my sexual abuse makes my gut hurt. In many ways my relationships, when it comes to sex and intimacy, have been incapacitated. I have a very difficult time trusting the opposite sex and, to be honest, I am terrified of being sexual. I didn't come out about my abuse until I was in my mid-twenties and haven't talked about it much until now, in this book. Healing from the effects of childhood sexual trauma is a work in progress that I will touch on in a later chapter.

The initial years of my life shaped me. Do I wish things would have been a little different? I can't answer that question. I believe things happened exactly as they were supposed to happen. The Universe has been my school, and every encounter has been my lesson. Because of my childhood and my mother, I have strength and perseverance. I was the first to graduate from college in my family. I am financially secure. I am a hard worker. I've learned to believe in myself and pursue my dreams. Also, I feel I am one of the lucky ones growing up within the disease of Alcoholism because it led me to Alanon, a 12-step recovery program for friends and family of alcoholics. I have been a grateful member of Alanon for over 11 years and I adhere to a really strong program by attending Alanon meetings, reading the Alanon literature, being of service at meetings and working the steps with a sponsor. Living in the circumstances I did growing up, I learned to accept myself and to love myself through Alanon. Just for today, I deeply and completely love and accept myself as I am and with the life I was born into.

Came to Believe is about my spiritual journey. It tells the story of when I had a shift in my thinking. It is about recognizing that a power greater than myself knew what was best for me and guided me to see the Light and to be the Light. I can share about the miracles that unfolded for me because of my shift in perception from fear to love. *Came to Believe* is about manifesting my dreams, my strong connection with the angels and the healing work I was guided to do, once I became willing. It tells a story of how true forgiveness can heal. It's my memoir of when I came to believe.

Chapter Two
I Can See Clearly Now

"I am determined to see."
-A Course in Miracles

I believe in psychics. They have always intrigued me. The first psychic I saw was in New York City when I was in my early thirties. I love New York City. There is an energy there that is nowhere else! This woman didn't have a flashing "Psychic Readings" sign in her window; She was referred to me by someone I knew who I worked with me in the fashion industry. When I walked into her building, she greeted me wearing a white nightgown. Her hair was messy and stuck to her face because of the New York humidity. I was in awe of her. I resonated with her. She put my hands in hers and stared at me. She told me I was a New Yorker in my previous life and that I was psychic. Well, that wasn't the first time I had heard that, the being psychic part. She also told me that I was going to meet my soul mate and his initials would be G.R. That last part hasn't happened that I know of. It may have happened if I was open to meeting someone. But, at that moment I wasn't open to receiving love from a man.

Nine years later I saw another psychic in 2014. She was employed at a local metaphysical shop in Pasadena, California, called Alexandria II. I went to their website and looked at all the pictures and biographies of the psychics. I was drawn to Ambika. Her picture looked like an angel. In person, she was much more magnetic and magical. She had been a clairsentient, clairaudient and clairvoyant since she was a child. She could hear, feel and see angels, spirits and guides. She also dealt with childhood trauma. I booked 30 minutes with her right away. When we first met, I was mesmerized by her. She had long flowing gray hair, friendly dimples, and beautiful eyes that I felt reading me from the instant she started to walk towards me. I immediately thought she must be an amazing mother. In this session, she was able to pinpoint that I had grown up in an alcoholic home, I had psychic gifts, had a bright, colorful aura, and I had a ton of angels.

She laughed, "Wow, you have so many angels around you!" She specifically mentioned Aurora of the Northern Lights. From Doreen Virtue's Messages from your Angels Oracle Cards, the Aurora card says, "You are flying high right now, which may threaten others. But don't descend, because others will soon become inspired by your example." What she told me didn't make sense to me then, but it does now.

She also mentioned that my root chakra was unbalanced. She said I was living through my crown chakra and too attached to the Divine. "I can see the trauma and turmoil swirling about in your stomach, and it is going to come to a head, but you will see the light." She asked me to put my bare feet on the earth for 15 minutes a day to ground myself. For those of you who are not aware of the chakra system, the root chakra is the first chakra, and identified by the color red. It is located at the base of the spine and connects us to the physical world. It gives us a sense of safety and security with ourselves and others which stems from our childhood. It is governed by the spinal column, back, kidneys, legs, and feet. When the root chakra is out of balance, you could have bladder issues, lower back injuries, and problems with your feet. From the first chapter of this book, you found out that I wasn't grounded as a child, so everything that Ambika said made sense to me.

My mom came to visit me three weeks later from Phoenix, Arizona. We both love the beach, so I decided to take her to Broad Beach in Malibu, the perfect spot to place my Pisces feet in the sand and let the refreshing ocean water wash over me. I could ground myself and work on my root chakra as per

the psychic. There was a steep stairway with about
200 stairs heading down to Broad Beach and on this
day, it was covered with debris from a storm.
California had El Nino type storms the week prior, so
the beach was a mess! The stairway was rickety,
unsafe with handrails only on one side. I was
worried about my mom getting down the stairs as
she had bad knees. I had my adorable Shih Tzu,
Chester, in my arms along with about four bags to
carry down to the beach. I wanted my mom's hands-
free so she could walk safely down.

When we reached nearly the bottom of the stairs, I had my mom move in front of me so I could keep my eyes on her and I set Chester down. I looked out at the beach. The water sparkled. There wasn't anyone else on the beach except for another couple having a picnic. I went to take my next step and slipped on the sand between my flip-flop and the wood boarded walkway. I fell flat, fast and hard. I was in excruciating pain. I started to cry and scream. Whatever I injured hurt terribly! What had I done? I landed on my back that had previous injuries from a job accident and three car accidents. I had major lower back issues, hence the Root Chakra again. I wasn't sure exactly what I had hurt. I thought it was my back at first or maybe I injured my hands. I used them to try to protect my back when I landed. My ankle had twisted behind my back, and I was sitting on it when I landed. And then the pain started to pierce through, and I realized I had done something to my foot or ankle.

"Tara??!! What happened? Are you ok?" My mom looked worried. I couldn't respond. I just kept screaming and crying. I have never felt physical pain like that. I looked up and saw Chester. He was frightened and jumping on me, whimpering.

"Mom, pick up Chester!!!" I screamed at her. She called Chester over to her and picked him up.

"Tara, you okay? Where are you hurt?" She asked me again.

"I don't know," I managed to spit out at her in between the tears. I kept moaning in agony and breathing through clenched teeth. Did I actually sprain my ankle? I used my hands to bring my ankle out that was twisted from underneath me. I hoped that it was just an insignificant sprain and that the pain would subside, and I would walk it off like I used to do in softball many times.

"What should we do?" My mom looked as scared as Chester. She wasn't used to seeing me in this state. I was the strong one. She usually differed to me on things like this. In 2006, I had a breast reduction, and my mom flew out from Arizona to take care of me. She struggled to see me so out of it and not in control. I could only imagine what she was thinking now as I laid there unable to understand what in the heck had happened, through my tears and agony. I don't remember the last time I had cried that much and hard. My face burned from my tears.

"I don't know. Let's just get down to the beach and enjoy our picnic." There was still about a five feet drop with sand bags to get down to set up a picnic out on the sand. Sure, Tara, that sounded like the logical thing to do! Simply ignore the fact you severely injured yourself, brush it off and act like nothing happened. I apparently messed up my ankle pretty badly, yet was more concerned with making sure I didn't ruin the beach day, typical behavior from an adult child of an alcoholic. I looked around the beach and was freaking out. What the hell was I going to do?

The husband of the couple on the beach came over to assist me. "Can I help?" he asked. "I'm sorry I didn't come over sooner, I thought you were laughing; then my wife told me to check on you. She thought it was serious." I asked him if he could carry me down to the beach so we could have our picnic.

"Don't you think we should call an ambulance?" He suggested. I didn't want to do that. I had my car, my mom and Chester. My mom barely drives and would not be able to navigate the Los Angeles freeways on her own. I knew in my heart there was no way I was driving myself, my mom and my precious Shih Tzu back to Pasadena, but I wasn't willing to submit quite yet. I hoped it would go

away; we could have our picnic and then head back.
I was delusional! Who in their right mind would
think that? My ankle was ballooning up by the
minute all the way down to my toes. It looked bad.
My toes were now sausages.

"Just carry me down, please?" I was still
whimpering. I tried to mask my tears in front of this
stranger. I didn't want him to see me weak. He tried
to get me up and he couldn't. I couldn't get myself
up. I was powerless. He finally was able to get me up
with my Mom's help and suggested bringing me
down to the water to soak my foot. "The cold water
might help with the swelling," he suggested. He
carried me down and laid me near the surf. In two-
seconds, a wave came crashing in and took me out! I
was soaked and covered in sand.

I began to shriek, "Oh my God, please help me."
The pain was paralyzing. The kind man, Bryan,
helped pull me up the beach with my ankle banging
on the sand along the way. He seemed freaked out
by my behavior and didn't know how to help
someone who was impossible to help. He went back
to his wife. I merely laid there crying and screaming.
My mom tried to rationalize with me to call 911.

I kept yelling at her, "Do something! Be the adult for once!" I was extremely rude and mean to her. What was she supposed to do? I wasn't giving her any answers. 911 was the best call for salvation. I remember trying to push myself up, and I saw Chester running along the beach chasing this couple's pet Iguana? I couldn't make this up. I felt I was in crazy town. And the only one acting crazy was me!

Being the control freak that I am, I dialed 911, not my mom. She wouldn't know how to tell them where we were. I wasn't even sure how to describe where we were. I didn't even trust her to "do something" so simple. I let the 911 operator know what happened and gave the best location I could. We were in such a remote area in Malibu that the ambulance had a hard time finding our exact location when they arrived. They had to acquire permission to get through a private residential gated area to find us. The paramedics left the ambulance at the top of the cliff and ran down the driveway closest to where we were, avoiding the 200 plus stairs down the cliff. There were about five paramedics all firing a multitude of questions at me. I couldn't answer any of them. I wasn't able to focus because of the pain, crying and moaning. I was in total shock. My mother even told me that one of the paramedics asked if I was always this dramatic? My mom said, never, that I usually hold everything together and get through it. That was sweet of her to say.

The couple came back over to help with Chester and my mom. The wife, Angie could tell I was more worried about the two of them than myself. She immediately stepped right in and consoled them like an angel. The paramedic informed me that this was one of the worst ankle injuries he had seen in a while, and they are called to that very same spot often for falls on those stairs. I didn't fall on the stairs, I waited to slip once I got to the flat surface! He told me that I would need to head to the emergency room.

"What about my mom and Chester? I have my car here." The paramedic said my mom would have to drive my car home. He didn't understand. My mom couldn't do it. Again, I thought she couldn't fix things or even take care of me. I was in a complete panic. What the heck would I do?

The paramedic said, "You are going to have to calm down and just breathe. Can you breathe in deep for me and then exhale it out? Keep doing that and close your eyes." Angie offered to drive my mom and Chester home while we rushed to the emergency room. The couple lived in Montrose and Pasadena was on the way. What were the odds of that? It was a miracle. I couldn't stop crying and thanking her. Seriously, I do not know what we would have done if it weren't for her. I guess my mom and Chester would have come with me to the hospital in the ambulance, and I would have figured out how to get my car later. At the time, I never thought to ask my Higher Power to step in. *A Course in Miracles* says, "When you are in the presence of fear, you are relying on your own strength." I was afraid. I was freaking the *f* out.

I met Angie and her husband Bryan for lunch today about a year and a half after the accident. I had met Angie for lunch before about four months after the traumatizing event to thank her too. It was fun to have both of them at lunch today. When I met Bryan, this time, I asked, "What does it feel like to meet the lady who screamed and cried for hours as you tried to save her?" He laughed and reminded me that it was a pretty scary accident. They let me know that they were going to go to Manhattan Beach on the day of the accident, but decided at the last minute to go to Broad Beach in Malibu. It was wonderful to see them and talk about that crazy day.

Angie told me that when I first fell she asked Bryan, "Please check on her, I don't think she is okay. She sounds like she is in a lot of pain." She also told me today that she felt so bad for me because she knew that all I was looking to do was have a nice picnic with my mom. They have also inherited two more pet Iguanas for a total of three! I will never forget Angie and Bryan and what they did for me. I know we will stay in touch forever and today I can see they were my angels stepping in for me when I couldn't do for myself.

The paramedics had to persuade me to get on the stretcher and to be carried up those 200 stairs. It was pretty horrible being elevated upside down while in terrifying pain. I had never been more fearful in my life. I was hyperventilating. I couldn't catch my breath. To make things more stressful, we couldn't find the keys to my car for Angie to drive my mom home. "Mom, just find my keys!" There I was screaming at her again. She eventually found them in my purse that I tucked away in one of the beach bags.

The paramedics put me in the ambulance, and I was on my way to the hospital while my mom rode with Angie and Chester back to Pasadena. I sobbed the entire ambulance ride to the hospital. The nearest hospital was 25 miles away, and it was right in the middle of Los Angeles traffic on the 101 Freeway Northbound. I was stuck in this ambulance and felt like all the air on earth had escaped me. The paramedic continued to urge me to breathe. He said he would have to put an oxygen mask on me if I couldn't relax. I couldn't stop crying. I was alone in the ambulance, and I wished my mom was with me. I closed my eyes and prayed. I prayed to whoever would listen to restore me to sanity. I began "Breath of Fire." Breath of Fire is rapid and continuous breath through the nostrils with the mouth closed. It is equal on the inhale and the exhale, with no pause between them. Breath of Fire strengthens the nervous system to reduce stress and anxiety. I learned this in my Kundalini Yoga class. I slowly began to calm down. I focused my eyes on a third eye point and settled into this long ride to the hospital. The third eye point is your inner wisdom, also known as your intuition. It is the lens beyond your physical sight. As I was breathing, I saw a crazy light show in my third eye of green and blue lasers. It was magnificent.

A calmness then settled over me, and I heard a voice that said, "You are ok. Don't worry. Tara, breathe." I felt like someone had hugged me. I later learned this was Archangel Raphael and Archangel

Michael. Archangel Raphael is the angel of healing and is identified by the color green. Archangel Michael is the angel of protection and is identified by the colors royal blue and gold.

Before I knew it, we were at the hospital! It was my first time in the emergency room. Surprisingly, after my unruly behavior earlier, I was calm. I was brought into the emergency room and X-rays were taken right away. It had been hours since I'd been able to use the bathroom and I had to go. The nurses wouldn't let me. They were worried I would injure myself more by getting up. They offered me a bed pan, but I said no thank you. I had used a bed pan previously during my myomectomy surgery and it wasn't pretty.

The doctor came in then. "Wow, what did you do?" I told him the story. The short version, leaving out the bits where I was screaming, crazy and was rude to my Mother. "I haven't seen a break this bad in a while." Thanks, doctor. Way to make me feel better.

He told me my right ankle was broken in three spots and that I would need surgery right away. I had never broken anything in my 38 years of life. When I was little, I always wished I would so I could

have a cool cast that all my friends would then sign.
"I don't have an orthopedic surgeon on staff right
now. Do you have one that you could get into
tomorrow?" Um, no. I don't even have a ride home
from this place.

Thank goodness for iPhones and Breath of Fire.
I closed my eyes and started the breath work again. I
then began to Google orthopedic surgeons in
Pasadena. I was tremendously grateful for the
internet, Google and iPhones. I also called my
insurance company to get some names of doctors.
Of course, being the control freak I am, I "Yelped"
them all to see who had the best reviews. This was
my ankle we were talking about, and I wasn't about
to see someone who had bad reviews. I found the
perfect doctor and had an appointment for the next
day! I also found a ride home from the hospital, too.
My wonderful cousin, Jen, was going to drive from
Rancho Cucamonga, California all the way to West
Hills, California, to save me. I had so much gratitude
at that moment. Grateful for Angie, for the
paramedics, for my mom, this orthopedic surgeon I
hadn't met yet, and for my cousin. At that time, I
don't think I would have credited the angels for
resolving all the details, but I do now.

Chapter 3
Angels? Are You There? It's Me.

"Came to believe that a power greater than ourselves could restore us to sanity."
-Alanon Second Step

I was truly miserable sitting in the Emergency Room, drenched and sandy from the beach. They had forced my ankle straight and wrapped it tightly with me screaming the entire time. I was so disruptive that the doctor came rushing back in to check on me, "Are you ok?" Through my tears, I said, "It hurts when they are forcing it straight." The doctor informed the nurse to wrap it the way it was. I was such a drama queen!

I still had to pee. My bladder was about to burst open. My urge to go was exactly like in the Detrol commercials, "Gotta go, Gotta go, Gotta go right now." The nurse eventually allowed me to use the restroom. They helped me into a wheelchair and rolled me down the hall. This was when things got even more interesting. My clothes were sopping wet and filled with sand. At some point, I lost my flip flops. I reached into my pockets to release the sand and crabs, yes; live crabs scattered across the bathroom floor trying to find sand to disappear in.

Those tiny guys made it all the way with me through the ambulance ride to the emergency room. Sand was everywhere. I destroyed that restroom. I was embarrassed, but I had to laugh! It was funny and was going to make for an excellent story later!

I called the nurse back in. "Um, there are crabs and sand all over your bathroom floor." I am sure I had a cheeky grin on my face. She smiled.

"Crabs? Now that is something I have never seen before. I have been an emergency room nurse for 20 years," she laughed and somehow I was proud of myself for making her day.

My cousin arrived at the hospital after I'd been there for four hours. I was freezing and wishing I had some warm clothes to put on. It took me a while to figure out how to get in her car without hitting my ankle or being in complete agony. The car ride home was 40 miles and took about two hours with traffic, typical in Los Angeles. I could not wait to get home. I called my mom on the ride home to check in. She could not stop talking about Angie, my angel.

"Angie asked me if I believed in angels. I started to cry," my mom said. This was when I truly felt in my soul that angels existed. I mean real life angels in the flesh. I got the chills. Angie and her husband were the only other people on the beach that day. They lived in Montrose, California, which was only a short distance past Pasadena going northwest on the 210 freeway. She drove my mom and Chester home in my new car while her husband followed. I didn't even question this couple with a pet iguana, which I had never met before, taking my mom and my dog and driving my brand-new car. I had to believe that they were going to be protected, and they were! Archangel Michael was with them too, I realized. If Angie and Bryan were not there that day, I have no idea how I would have survived this. Then again, if they were not there that day I don't think my mother, and I would have made the trip to Broad Beach. We may have gone to Manhattan Beach where Angie and Bryan had originally planned to go.

After my cousin had left, my mom and I enjoyed our beach picnic in my apartment. The sandwich was soggy, but it didn't matter. I was just grateful to be home to see Chester and my mom safe in my apartment. I wasn't going to be able to relax until I knew they were okay. I couldn't get around my place at all. I was on crutches, which was also a first for me. Using crutches is quite difficult when used correctly. It exhausted me getting from one room to the next. I kept telling myself, "Girl, keep working those crutches and you will get Madonna's arms."

At that moment, I was dependent, something I hadn't experienced since I was a very small child. Being reliant on another person was the most uncomfortable feeling for me. I've heard before that it's hard to get comfortable with being uncomfortable, but when you do, amazing things happen. As Mom and I enjoyed our apartment picnic, we talked about the day. I asked her, "Why did this happen to me? What is the lesson here?" Then I remembered what the psychic in Pasadena had said, "Your Root Chakra is out of balance. Everything is swirling about, and it's going to come to a head soon, and you will see the light."

"Oh my God! Mom, this is exactly what the psychic was talking about," I blurted out as it hit me! Root Chakra and a broken ankle; things must have "come to a head." I was starting to connect the dots. I have learned that the root chakra is directly related to the lack of safety and security during childhood. I resonated with that completely. Often, I did not feel safe in my home and always worried about financial security.

My mom was due to fly out the next day to go home. We decided to cancel her flight. Instead, her boyfriend and their little dog, Annabelle, drove out from Arizona to help. I felt a tremendous amount of guilt for him coming and my mom staying. Money was tight for them. The amount her boyfriend had to pay for the gas to drive out here, him missing work, her missing work, all weighed on me. Partially, because I felt I would have to give them money to compensate, and this unnerved me. I have helped my mother a few times financially, and I always felt this made our relationship muddy. It made our roles confusing. Most children wouldn't have to pay their parents to take care of them when they were injured. This burden I was feeling was mine. I later learned it was all in my head. It was old stuff that I needed to release. My mom wasn't expecting money from me; that was my extreme need to care take jumping in when it wasn't necessary.

I had trouble sleeping that first night, so much was running through my head. The accident, my angel Angie, the iguana, Chester terrified on the beach at my screaming, the pain and the way I had treated my mom. I couldn't get comfortable with this huge bandage suffocating my extremely swollen ankle, foot and toes. I tossed and turned all night thinking about everything. Angie kept coming to my mind. Was she an angel? Did God send her to me? Again, in my head, I repeated, "Angie and Bryan were the only other folks on this beach. They lived just past Pasadena. They had intended to go to Manhattan Beach, not Broad Beach." Her name was Angie, the Latin name is *Angelus*, which derives from a heavenly creature. The Greek name for Angela is *Angelos*, which means messenger. (from www.behindthename.com) I now know that Angie was sent to me from Archangel Ariel and Archangel Michael to protect me in nature and save my mom, Chester and me from this situation. I had mentioned earlier that Archangel Michael is the angel of protection. Archangel Ariel is a healing angel, as well as a protector of nature.

I knew a little bit about angels prior to the accident because two months before and one month before seeing the psychic I came in contact with my first deck of Angel Oracle Cards by Doreen Virtue. I was having lunch with one of my closest girlfriends, Marina. We were at Urth Cafe in Pasadena, and it was such a beautiful day outside. The sun felt warm and healing against my skin. I was telling her all about the financial situation I was in with my mom, and as usual, she was an excellent listener with no judgments. I was in the middle of filing for bankruptcy. I was embarrassed about it at the time because I was financially responsible when it came to my own affairs. I didn't want anyone to know about it, so I rarely shared it with anyone. Bankruptcy has such a negative connotation to it. People who file for bankruptcy are judged to be irresponsible. I had a lot of shame about it.

The reason I had to file was because when I was in my early twenties, I signed for a house for Mom to help her get out of a bad boyfriend situation. I didn't understand what I was doing. At first, I thought I was simply co-signing, but apparently, I was the only signer on the loan. It didn't matter because both were equally terrible. It was a thirty-year loan for $35,000 for a manufactured home. 18 years later, we had paid $82,000 towards a $35,000 loan and still owed $30,000. I know. Horrible! It thoroughly disgusted me thinking about it. Also, 18 years later the manufactured home was deteriorating. The whole thing was breaking and falling apart. I had talked to my mom about moving out of it, but I didn't want to make her feel like I was kicking her out. The only thing to do was to walk away from this house and mortgage payment. I couldn't afford the repairs. My mom's Social Security and her part-time job provided barely enough income for her to live there. The house stressed me out. The financial responsibility of it contributed to my mom's and my relationship being unbalanced. I wasn't her landlady, and if she didn't have the money to pay the mortgage, it was on my credit. This situation caused me a lot of sleepless nights.

To be honest, what caused me the most anxiety was the thought of Mom dying and me having to clean out the house and figure out what to do with it. She had years of belongings accumulated in that home. I thought it was her responsibility to help me with this. I asked her if she would help me clean everything out and move in with her boyfriend. She agreed. I came to Arizona, and my oldest adopted brother, my mom and I cleaned out the house and storage shed. We filled four truckloads of stuff to the Goodwill and filled up at least ten big trash cans. I was proud of my mom. She labored hard to get this done. She knew it was important to me. She slowly moved carload by carload over to her new home. I knew my mom was nervous about moving into her boyfriend's place, but she did it to help me out of this situation. In a way, I felt it was her amends to me. I was grateful to my mom's boyfriend for letting my mom move in. It was a win-win situation because he had wanted her to move in for a while. Once she moved out, the next step was for me to file bankruptcy to get rid of the house and the awful creditor.

After lunch Marina and I walked over to my favorite bookstore, Vroman's in Pasadena to look around. I always gravitated to the metaphysical, new age section. I saw this box of cards on a spinning rack. There were a ton of cards by different authors. I picked up a purple deck, as purple is my favorite color. The box said they were Daily Guidance by your Angels Oracle Cards by a woman named Doreen Virtue. I opened up the box. Marina was wandering around in another section. I closed my eyes, and I started to mix them up. I didn't shuffle them like a card deck, I mixed them up in my hands, splitting them differently each time, which isn't how I shuffle the cards now when I do readings.

I took a deep breath and said, "Ok, what do you want to tell me, Angels?" I felt a sensation to stop shuffling. The feeling I got to stop shuffling was clairsentient, a gift which I later learned I have. Clairsentient is a "clear feeling" and is an extremely heightened form of empathy. My insights, instincts and gut feelings have always been on point when it comes to situations and people. Now, when I am using angel cards, I get a sense from the angels of when to stop shuffling the cards to provide accurate guidance. I drew the top card, "Shower of Abundance." The card said, "To heal your financial situation, first give us your worries concerning

45

money. We will guide you in order to show you how to create and accept abundance. As we work together, your financial situation will heal as fast as you allow it." I felt a wave of heat go over me. That feeling was relief and assurance that I was watched over by spirit. I turned the box over to see how much these cards were. $15? Not bad, so I went straight away to the cashier to pay for them. The bankruptcy went perfect, and there were no issues. My credit score is almost right back where it was.

I started to do readings for my friends and study every book I could get my hands on from Doreen Virtue and about angels. My readings for my friends were amazingly accurate, that for the first time I started to believe in my connection to the angels and my spiritual gifts. I had been very intuitive as a child, and several psychic experiences had happened to me growing up, but I never talked about them. My mom was an astrologer, so I grew up learning about astrology. She had taken me to an astrologer when I was a child and was told that I was very psychic and that she should watch out for that. I am a Pisces. If you are a Pisces, it is normal to feel super spiritual and have an excellent intuition. Pisces are also more likely to surrender to something outside of themselves for guidance. (from www.tarot.com) It was no accident that those Oracle Cards presented themselves to me that day. I went to see the psychic Ambika, who confirmed I had these gifts and predicted my spiritual awakening a month after buying the angel cards. Nor was it an accident that Angie and her husband were on the beach that day when I broke my ankle with my mom gifting me what I know now was a Spiritual Awakening. It was Divine intervention. I now have more than 30 decks of angel, tarot and oracle cards and give readings to clients all over the world. I will get into this later in the book.

Chapter 4
You Will See the Light

"Be the peace you are seeking from others. If peace is missing in your relationships with your family, it means that you have a place within you that is occupied by non-peace."
-Dr. Wayne Dyer

My mom came from my room, "I made your bed, but I am sure it's not to your expectations." It's true, I was pretty OCD (obsessive compulsive disorder) and had to have everything in its place. I had finished telling her that she missed some spots on my floor when she was sweeping it for me right before she made my bed. It would have driven me crazy to stare at those spots on the floor from my recliner chair and not be able to do anything about it.

"I am sure it is fine, mom," I brushed her off.

"You don't seem like you want us here," she questioned me.

"Why do you say that?" I questioned right back.

"You don't seem to appreciate us being here." Wow. Honestly? I didn't appreciate her? I have done so much for my mother most of my life. I took care of things for her, even when her alcoholism affected me. I was always there. I never gave up on her. I always had hoped she would get sober. I believed I could get her sober. Through Alanon, I learned that it wasn't up to me. My mom has her own Higher Power, as do all of us. I couldn't be my mom's Higher Power.

"I don't appreciate you?" I screamed. "Are you kidding me? I have done everything for you. You don't appreciate me!" "Everything," was a slight exaggeration.

"Tara, you act like you don't want us here." She replied, staring at me with no reaction about how much she had obviously triggered me.

"Then leave! You guys can go home. I can figure out my ride to the surgery. I will take care of Chester myself; I do not need you." I shouted through my tears. I was thoroughly enraged and tired. I tried to lift myself out of the chair with my crutches, and I struggled. It was incredibly hard to get up on my own. How was I going to manage Chester after I had now kicked them out? I would figure it out as I

50

always did. I'd be damned if I'd take my mom's help after she said I didn't appreciate her. I was very stubborn. I got up and spastically made it to my room, with Chester while on my crutches. I slammed the door. I picked Chester up on to the bed and laid down with my boy.

"I'm sorry, buddy, did I scare you? I love you so much, Chester." I was crying. Dogs are always wonderfully sensitive; he clearly knew I was upset. He came up to my face and started to lick my tears. "You will be a good boy and make it easy for mommy to take care of you?" He stared at me with his big brown eyes and long eyelashes licking my salty and teary-eyed face. This dog is my everything. I got him when I was thirty, and I have been obsessed with him ever since. He has been my spiritual running buddy.

My mom came into my room to try to reason things out with me. I yelled, "Get out! Get your shit out of here and leave! I don't want you here." How cruel I was to say that. As I am typing this, it brings an enormous amount of emotion out of me. It was a mean and disgusting thing to say to my mother. I cannot believe such hate came out of my mouth. It was apparently from all those years and years of resentment.

"Tara, what is the matter? Why are you so upset?" She didn't understand that all the years of resentment that I had bottled up inside me suddenly came to the surface. I would never let her know about how her drinking affected me because I didn't want to upset her. All my emotions came to a head, exactly as Ambika, my psychic, had said.

"I have always taken care of you and been there for you! How can you say I don't appreciate you when you don't appreciate me? I was always the one who stood by you! I was the mother." My face was red and smeared with snot and tears. "Get out!" She left my room.

Could I take care of Chester? I would have to go down a few stairs three times a day to take him out potty. I decided to try it. I grabbed him off the bed to put him on the floor, then left my room. "Come on buddy, let's go potty." The good news was Chester followed me everywhere I went, literally everywhere, he especially loved joining me in the bathroom. I am never worried about him running off.

My mom asked me where I was going? "What do you care?" I went outside, and I collapsed. I couldn't do it. Chester ran away because the crutches crashing on the floor scared him. I hung on to the wall. How was it going to be after the surgery? No doubts, it was going to be much worse. I was defeated. I was embarrassed. I was dependent. I hated being dependent upon anyone. I could take care of myself and had for so many years. I sobbed.

"Chester, Come on! Let's go inside." He usually needed help up the stairs because he is partially blind and his vision is primarily affected when its dark outside. I left him at the bottom of the steps, he pleaded with me to help him, and I couldn't. He whined and whimpered. It broke my heart. I was going to have to go back inside and ask my mom for help. That was going to kill me after the way I treated her. It broke my heart seeing Chester desperate to come up the stairs and to be with his upset mommy. "Grandma will get you," I assured him.

After kneeling down on my good leg to grab my crutches, I went back inside and asked my mom to get Chester. I returned to my room and slammed the door, again. I was surprised by my dramatic behavior. I usually did not get this upset about things. I'd always stuffed my feelings for fear of them affecting someone else. Something I learned early on; not to talk, trust or feel. I got back in bed and thought to myself, "Now what am I going to do? I am fucked."

My mom knocked on the door. "Tara, let me come in." She pushed the door open and came to my bed with Chester. My face burned. I was slightly sunburned, so the tears were sizzling on my face. I couldn't look at her. "Tara," she called again. She grabbed my hand. "I'm your mother. I love you. I want to take care of you." That broke me. I surrendered. She started to cry. I was already crying. "I didn't know you felt that way. I am sorry." This was the apology I had been waiting for.

We hugged each other, and I kept crying loudly. These were tears that have wanted to fall for years. I didn't say I was sorry for the things I said. I just hugged my mom. "Come out and sit with us," she said. I told her I would be out in a minute. I was deeply embarrassed; how could I go out there? I took some deep breaths, wiping my face with my sheets. I opened my door, hesitated, and went out to the living room with my crutches.

"Sorry," I said to my mom's boyfriend. He was always so sweet and understood the family disease of alcoholism. He has been in Alcoholics Anonymous for many years and had told me some of his own stories from his disease. I made my way to the chair to sit down, and my mom put Chester on my lap.

"I'm going to miss you, little guy, when Grandma takes you home with her." I rubbed his ears and chin, one of his favorite things. My mom was taking Chester home to Arizona for six weeks while I recuperated from the surgery. When I called a friend a few months after the accident to fess up about my poor behavior with my mother she asked me, "How much would it have cost you to have someone take care of Chester for six weeks?" She was right; it would have cost me over $1000 to take him to a pet sitter. And I knew my mom loved Chester. She took excellent care of him, and he is happy with her. He got to sleep with her. She gave him treats for when he went potty, even though he has been potty trained since he was three months. Yes, he still demands treats after potty, and he is 11 now. Her watching Chester for six weeks was a gift.

The next day was the surgery, and we had to be at the Hospital at 5:30 am. I have had surgery before, and every time it's a scary feeling to be put to sleep beforehand. I had decided to stay overnight at the hospital to give myself a break from Mom and her boyfriend and give my mom a break from me. I wanted to be able to sleep with no distractions. I am such a people pleaser that I knew by going home right away I wouldn't relax and would try to do things and fix things. At the time, my self-care practice definitely had room for improvement.

The last thing I remember before surgery was telling my mom that I loved her and that everything will be ok. As I was rolling back to the operating room, my doctor asked me what music I would like to listen to during the surgery.

"I won't hear it, right?" I laughed. I chose a pop channel, of course! I think I specifically said, "Any Madonna?" I have been a huge Madonna fan since High School. She was a role model for me in the 90's, full of power and perseverance. Her success and strength inspired me. My doctor put on "Ray of Light," one of my favorites of her songs. The lyrics were fitting, "Quicker than a ray of light, she's flying, trying to remember how it all began."

The anesthesiologist came in and started talking to me about the process of being put under, and I began to panic. He held my hand and said not to worry that I wouldn't remember a thing, with a chuckle. First, they did the block in my right leg at the knee down, and two-seconds later the anesthetic kicked in through the IV. I could feel it all happening. Once the anesthetic started, I felt it burning through the IV. I remember saying, "It burns." And then I was out.

I woke up from surgery, and my mom was right there by my side. I was thirsty, but they wouldn't let me drink anything. I was only allowed ice chips. I needed to pee. Of course, I needed to pee. My timing for having to use the restroom was always horrible. My frequent urination problem made things difficult. I pee about twenty times a day, and the doctors have not been able to figure out why. I thought having a 5 1/2-inch fibroid tumor "baby" removed from my uterus in 2013 would have helped, but no dice. I still peed just as much. The nurse insisted I use the bedpan. Ugh, I get it. When I had a breast reduction back in 2006, I needed to pee once I woke up from surgery. The nurse told me I needed to use the bed pan. I told her, "No." I wasn't very good at following orders back then. I have been told I was a non-compliant patient by several doctors. I got up and tried to walk to the bathroom and threw up all over the hospital floor. Therefore, when this nurse insisted, this time, I obliged. Peeing in a bedpan in front of your mother is really something! "Mom, turn around and don't look."

I said goodbye to my mom and was ready to relax and sleep in my hospital room for 24 hours of silence and comfort with someone waiting on me hand and foot. The pain wasn't too bad at first. The leg block was still in effect. They offered me Morphine, but I rejected it. I told the nurse, "The last time when I was given Morphine was when my huge fibroid tumor was removed. It made me crazy." She was concerned and grateful for my honesty. When I had my fibroids removed, I was in the hospital for three days. I became attached to that Morphine handheld device thing. If you aren't familiar, when you are on morphine in the hospital, they try to regulate it by giving you a handheld device. You can only have more by pushing the button when the light turns blue. I kid you not, every time the light turned blue I pushed the button for more. When the head nurse tried to take it away from me, I started to scream at her, "Nooooo, I need it! You don't understand!" I was insane! She scolded me like an addict, and I reacted like an untreated addict. I had to make amends to her on checkout day. Not only that, it made me horribly sick once I got home. I was so nauseous that I couldn't even walk. I felt horrible and all I could eat for days was saltine crackers and drink Ginger Ale. Instead, I decided to take Vicodin. Looking back, I'm not sure if that was any better of a decision. I have learned that Vicodin doesn't sit well in my tummy either.

I don't remember much from the hospital stay. I had difficulty sleeping as the nurse kept coming in to check on me. Before I knew it, my 24 hours were up, and my mom and her boyfriend were there to pick me up and take me home. We stopped by Target on the way home, to stock up on supplies and groceries since I knew I would not be leaving the house anytime soon. I couldn't drive for two months, and I certainly wasn't walking anywhere. I have always secretly wanted to ride one of the motorized carts at the stores, and now I had my chance! I remember my Mom and I laughing because I kept bumping into things, it was hilarious. I seemed in good spirits. I was excited to get home, put my feet up and watch endless hours of mindless television, numbing out what I was feeling underneath. Some people use drugs or alcohol; I use reality television. My reality was that I was worried about my mom. I knew she didn't feel good about leaving the next day. She was concerned about how I was going to get along. I was new to Pasadena. I didn't know anyone local to help me. I kept telling her, "I will be fine! Don't worry!" I was always fine.

I didn't know what to expect. My precious baby boy, Chester was going to be gone with my mom for two months. I was going to be alone. Let me take a second to explain how much Chester means to me. He is my baby. He is my rock and my best friend. I often tell him I gave birth to him and carried him in

my womb for nine months. And, I am not kidding! I
feel like this little guy is my gift from God. He came
to me exactly when I needed him. He is the first
thing I have taken care of by myself. He loves me
unconditionally, as long as I give him plenty of treats.
"You can't ever leave me; you are going to live
forever," I tell him. I ask him at least twenty times a
day, "Do you know how much mommy loves you?" I
usually respond to my question in a cute voice I
made for him. He is always there for me. He kisses
me before bedtime and to wake me up in the
morning. He is my everything. I even heard once
that an old co-worker of mine said to my other co-

worker, "Tara, is obsessed with her dog." After that, every post on Facebook or Instagram of my precious snowflake I use the hashtag, #iamobsessedwithChester. I know it's a lot of responsibility to put on a furry fellow, to "live forever." So, now I tell him that he is going to be one of Archangel Ariel's helpers to protect all the animals of the Universe and help them cross over. This way he can visit his mommy whenever he wants to. Archangel Ariel, as I mentioned earlier, is the protector of nature and animals.

It also made me a somewhat uneasy that I probably would not see another individual for a while as I would be secluded in my apartment. No co-workers to chat it up with, no Alanon meetings to go to and no friendly dogs with their owners to play with on my walk. I might not speak to another human being in the flesh for weeks! What was I going to do with my time? How was I going to get around my apartment? How would I make my food, shower, and water my gorgeous succulents outside my door? One of the only things I knew for sure was that I worked for an extraordinary company. I was being paid, and my job was protected while I was in recovery. All else was unknown, and I had to accept that. I did have a strong knowing that since my incident at the beach, meeting my angel, Angie, and with what my psychic told me of how many angels I had around me, I was in good hands. If I chose to pray and ask for help from my Higher Power and my Angels, I would get through this. I guess "this" is what the psychic meant when she said, "You will see the light." My light will be how I react to all that has happened to me when I sit with myself and my feelings for the next few months. The light was my connection with the Angels.

Chapter 5
What the Heck Is a Chakra?

"Giving up the need to know why something has happened to you will definitely count among the most rigorous personal challenges of your life."
-Caroline Myss

It was time for my mom, her boyfriend, Annabelle and Chester to leave for Arizona. I stood there in the driveway hanging over the crutches, leaning against a wall and gripping Chester as tightly as I could. I didn't want to let go of my boy to put him in the car. He knew something was up, and this always breaks my heart. My mom gave me a hug and assured me, "I love you, he will be fine!" She put Chester in the back seat with Annabelle. Chester jumped on the side window staring at me with those pleading eyes to not abandon him. It killed me inside to say goodbye to my little guy. I said bye to my mom's boyfriend and thanked him for driving out and turned back to go inside with tears streaming down my face. I felt alone. They had just driven away, and I already missed my mom and Chester. I struggled to my bed, laid down and cried uncontrollably. I wiped my tears with my sheets and closed my eyes. "Everything is going to be okay. I will survive," I said over and over until I believed it. Again, I saw flickers of yellow, gold and green light in my third eye point and within minutes I was asleep. Sometimes, I am not sure if these colors I see are the Archangels or the color of the chakras. Both Archangels and chakras have colors that help identify them. Whatever it is and whenever it happens, I now know it is spirit trying to connect with me. Green indicates Archangel Raphael, the angel of healing. Green also represents the Heart Chakra. Archangel Jophiel radiates the color yellow when present. Jophiel helps one to see their value and creates inspiration. The Third Chakra, the navel point, and solar plexus is also identified by the color yellow. For me when I see those colors of the chakras, it lets me know there is energy work to do in those areas.

Being emotionally and physically drained and having a mild case of depression, I slept for 15 hours after they left. I wasn't sure what depression felt like, as I often masked my feelings. I was lonely. I felt helpless. All I could do was cry. Whenever I do cry, or I am upset by something it opens up the floodgates and I go into a low vibration. I start to think about situations that I wished would have gone differently in my life. I start to ask, "Why would God do this?" I needed a change in attitude fast because I could see these feelings taking me down a path of darkness and destruction. I opened my eyes and looked at my God Box sitting on my dresser. Any time that I need to let go of something or need help from my angels or God, I write it down on a small piece of paper, fold it up and put the date on it. I then place it into my God Box. The act of putting the paper in the box is saying to my Angels and Higher Power, "I am ready to release this to you. My will is not sufficient. Please show me the way." I have used this box for seven years, and in the beginning, I referred to it as my God Box. I began to call my box my "Angel Box" after the ankle accident. My niece, when she was five, when visiting me one summer asked me what it was. I was nervous to tell her because I know her parents aren't into my "woo-woo" way of thinking. I just told her it was a God Box and when I worried about something I wrote it down and put it in the box. And told her by doing this, I was turning my worries over to God for help.

"Can I put something in it?" she asked me. I thought to myself, oh no, what could she possibly want to put in there? How was this going to get me in trouble with her father?

"What did you want to put in there?" I asked her.

She got shy, and she whispered, "Chevy." I started to tear up, but I didn't want her to see because I didn't want to scare her. Chevy is her first dog who passed away. She loved him so much. This dog allowed her to do whatever she wanted to him. Dress him up, crawl all over him, and walk him around the house on a leash.

"Ok baby, what did you want to say?"

"That God, please protect Chevy, so he doesn't die in Heaven," she said with such confidence.

I gave her a hug, "That is a very nice thing to ask for help with." I reassured her. Have I mentioned how much I love my niece? She is the daughter of my biological brother who is one year older than me. She is very special to me, and one of my favorite things to do is spend time with her. I wrote it down and let her put it in the box. It's funny because shortly after we did that, I went on a walk. While I was walking, my niece must have shown my mom the Angel Box. A few months after they left I was going through it, and I found my mom had put something in there too. She wrote, "My health." Those two entries from my mom and my niece are still in the box today.

I pushed myself out of bed and leaned over to the dresser to grab my Angel Box. I opened it up. I usually kept a pad of paper with angels on it that my mom bought for me and a pen. It makes it much easier to turn it over when I have all this stuff in the box, ready to go! I propped myself up with my pillows and took a deep breath. What did I want to turn over? I closed my eyes and took a few deep breaths, in and out. I was hoping to find those dancing colors in my third eye point again, but this time, it didn't happen. I did get an overwhelming feeling that everything was going to be okay. I opened my eyes and wrote down a few things:

1. Please help me to see the good in this situation.
2. Please help me not to feel sorry for myself.
3. Don't let me go without Starbucks for too long.

The last one, I was dead serious. I had Starbucks every day of my life for the last ten years. I had a serious Starbucks addiction. It's crazy to think of it today; I am caffeine free at the advice of Doreen Virtue. She told us in the Angel Intuitive course I took that caffeine and any stimulant interferes with one's connection to spirit and the angels. I believe this now, too, when it comes to caffeine. I haven't quite accepted that sugar also is a stimulant. I still love the taste of coffee, so when I do have it, I order decaf. I know what you are thinking, decaf has some caffeine in it. Progress not perfection. I believed by quitting caffeine that I would break up with Starbucks for good! Nope. It turns out I am also addicted to the stimulations I feel by having a handcrafted beverage in a pretty clear cup with a green straw. I am now striving to eliminate decaf coffee, as well, and I know I will kick this ritual to the curb! Sugar, I am also working on, slowly.

After putting those three items in my Angel Box, I said, "Thank you God and whoever else that has been looking out for me my entire life. I am grateful. I may be having a bit of a pity party now, but I am grateful." The thing is, I am glad I let myself feel those dark and depressed feelings. I needed to go into those dark corners and shine the light. A good cry always brings healing as I release that darkness. I sat on the side of my bed with my feet dangling over. This bandage cast thing was so big and ugly. I wanted to see what was underneath it. It took everything out of me to not take apart the bandage and have a look. I grabbed my crutches and moved slowly into the kitchen to make myself a bowl of cereal. Cereal is what I ate for every meal for about two months. It was the easiest to prepare and didn't require me to stand for too long. I remember crawling on the floor on my hands and knees while pushing the bowl of cereal across the floor to my recliner chair leaving my crutches in the kitchen. I couldn't use the crutches and hold my bowl of cereal at the same time.

Since I had this time off of work and could not move much, I decided to dive into some of the Self Help spiritual books that I had bought or borrowed. The first book I read was about chakras. I wanted to learn about my root chakra and figure out what exactly my psychic, Ambika, actually meant. And, what the heck was a chakra? According to www.suprapowers.com, the word chakra is derived from the Sanskrit word meaning "wheel." If we were able to see the chakras, we would observe a wheel of energy continuously revolving or rotating. Clairvoyants perceive chakras as colorful wheels or flowers with a hub in the center. The chakras begin at the base of the spine and finish at the top of the head. Though fixed in the central spinal column, the chakras are located on both the front and back of the body and operate through it. Each chakra vibrates or rotates at a different speed. The root or first chakra rotates at the slowest speed, the crown or seventh chakra at the highest speed. The first book I read was *Chakras for Beginners* by David Pond. Mr. Pond refers to the root chakra as the urge for survival. The root chakra is identified by the color red and is

69

located at the base of the tailbone. This first chakra is your connection with your body and Earth. It is how you survive. It is the center of safety and security that should have been provided to you in childhood. When this chakra is unbalanced, the way you view life may be confused with insecurities. This chakra also referred to as Muladhara, is the center of manifestation, where we are trying to make all our dreams happen in our material lives.

I have mentioned my upbringing earlier in the book, and by reading *Chakras for Beginners*, I learned that my root chakra was unbalanced because the lack of tribal instincts and familial bond growing up. My needs were often not met for one reason or another. Yes, I had basic shelter and food, but I didn't have a sense of self because I often emulated who I thought people wanted me to be. I was a peacekeeper, denying my desires and emotions to make sure everyone else was happy. My temperature matched my mother's. And as I said earlier, if she was sad, I was sad. If she was happy, I was happy. If she was depressed, I was depressed. We were enmeshed and co-dependent. As I mentioned, I didn't have a tight connection with my Dad. I saw my dad two times a week, but I never experienced having a father in the house. I do not even know what it is like to have an older male besides my brothers in the same house as my mother. So, you can imagine how everything was clicking together once I started to familiarize myself with my root chakra.

When the root chakra is out of balance, what happens? The next book I read was *Anatomy of the Spirit* by Caroline Myss. This book rocked my world. Here is what I learned, "To give up the need to know why things happen as they do." Basically, I needed to let go of the need to know why I was raised in a fatherless home, why I was affected by the disease of alcoholism, and why I broke my ankle in three spots on the beach with my mom. When the root chakra is out of balance, it can affect the health of your back, toes, immune system, rectum, and feet, according to *Anatomy of the Spirit.* Emotionally, it can affect the ability to stand up for yourself. Physically, it can cause obesity, anorexia, anxiety disorder/depression, feet problems, and chronic back pain. For me, it was my back, right ankle, and toes. In that order. I had a severe back injury on the job in 1999 before I even knew anything about spirituality, chakras, yoga or angels. This back injury has affected me continuously since then, but it also introduced me to one of my loves, yoga. I have been practicing yoga for 17 years. Since that injury, I was in three car accidents where I was rear-ended. You have already heard about my ankle accident, and after that I had multiple hammer toe surgeries on both feet two years in a row.

Coincidence? It all was becoming too fascinating to me. I decided to continue my research on my name after I started to see people post on social media pictures of White Tara and Green Tara angel cards. *Terra* means Earth in Latin. For someone whose name means Earth you would think they would be pretty grounded and that their root chakra was intact! The psychic also told me I was unbalanced to the crown chakra. The crown chakra is the last of the seven chakras. It gives us access to the higher consciousness, spirit and the Divine. It is identified by the color violet or purple. The crown chakra resonated with me, as I mentioned before, I was told when younger that I was very intuitive and had psychic qualities. When one is unbalanced to the crown chakra, they can often have headaches and feel confused. I have suffered from headaches since childhood. When I give too many angel card readings for clients in a row without a break, I get headaches too. My name also means *"star"* in Hindi. Tara is the name of a Hindu goddess, the goddess of peace and protection. Tara is also the name of the female Buddha in Buddhism. (All Tara facts are from www.wikipedia.com.) Star, Buddha, and the goddesses White and Green Tara seemed very related to the crown chakra. My mind was blown when I discovered this.

That simple, yet valuable, statement by Caroline Myss, "Give up the need to know why things happen as they do," changed my mindset from victim to a woman who can persevere! I was driving myself crazy trying to figure out why I'd had this ankle accident. Why would God do this to me? Caroline Myss also says, "Giving up the need to know why something has happened to you will definitely count among the most rigorous personal challenges of your life." I can see now that breaking my ankle was Divine timing, it was a Universal lesson so necessary to my spiritual growth. I learned that by always trying to answer the question of why, I was living in the past. I wasn't allowing myself to stay grounded or present. Now, I try to look at everything as an opportunity to learn and grow. Gabby Bernstein says, "Obstacles are detours in the right direction." I have had a lot of obstacles in my life and looking back, those obstacles gave me serious life cred. I trust that my angels and my Higher Power know what's best for me. When I put my faith in a power outside of myself, it gives me the opportunity just to breathe and enjoy each moment. I can do what I love and what honors my soul and spirit. I do not need to worry about anything.

Chapter 6
Daily Guidance from the Angels

"When we have faith in angels, they do deliver."
-Kyle Gray

I bought my first deck of Doreen Virtue Angel Oracle Cards after they practically jumped out at me in my local bookstore in Pasadena, Vroman's Bookstore, which I mentioned in Chapter Three. I strongly feel that those cards coming into my hands on that very day was a Divine intervention; they changed so much of my life. The confirmation that the bankruptcy was going to go well made me feel protected. I was extremely nervous about the bankruptcy. What if I was going to be stuck with that loan on a crumbling house? What would people think of me knowing that I had filed bankruptcy? Everything went smoothly, and no one judged me. I could not wait to play with these cards when I got home. I unpackaged the glowing, shiny purple box from its shrink wrap and took a deep breath. My mom had some tarot cards growing up, and I was drawn to them even then. The Daily Guidance from Your Angels was my very own first deck of cards from this woman, Doreen Virtue, whom I hadn't heard of until then. It made me laugh when I went to Hay House's and Doreen's Angel Intuitive Certification

Course in 2015, when she mentioned they were one of her favorite decks and perfect for beginners. At the end of the Angel Intuitive Course, she asked if anyone wanted the deck? I quickly shot my hand in the air and put on my biggest and brightest smile. She smiled back at me and gave me the deck. I was particularly appreciative because this was the deck of angel cards that had changed so much for me. I haven't opened the deck Doreen gave me since then. I wanted to keep it nice and new.

Little did I know how much this woman, Doreen Virtue, was going to influence my life. I looked at every single card and studied them. They were gorgeous. I didn't know how to use them, but I knew I loved them. I read the booklet that came with it, and it said to touch each card putting your energy and vibrations on it. I had already done that by admiring each card's artwork and inspiring messages. Then I learned I could ask the angels a one-card question or a three-card question. I decided to do another reading on myself asking, "Can I read angel cards?" I am laughing right now that this is what I decided to ask. You can tell at this time my confidence was lacking. I shuffled the cards like a dealer would in Vegas. I can only say that I just got a feeling of when to stop shuffling. That is my clairsentient abilities that I mentioned earlier. The card I pulled was "confidence." So, on point! The card read, "Moving forward does not necessarily require you to have confidence in yourself. Confidence in God is enough, along with knowing that God works through you and with you in all ways. Lean upon us if your confidence wavers and we will buoy your courage and faith." Well, then! It's true; I wouldn't have asked that question if I was confident. Also, if you remember, I specifically went and saw the psychic before my ankle accident to ask her if I could see angels and if I could do angel readings. I bought these cards in June 2015, and I saw the psychic in September 2015. Even though I asked the angels for validation in June 2015 with this deck, I still had to ask a real live psychic the same question in September 2015. My lack of confidence was getting in my own way of helping myself and others, through my connection with the angels.

I started to do readings for anyone who would let me! I brought the Daily Guidance from you Angel's deck with me everywhere I went. I consulted them for everything. Often, I just asked, "Angels, what do you have to tell me today?" The more I used them, the more confidence grew inside of me. I began receiving more and more angel messages without even using the cards. My friend, Jamie, who was my first friend in Pasadena when I moved here, believed in my mad angel skills. We met through a mutual friend and became close through our woo-woo ways. She recognized early on when we met that I was with spirit, so to speak. We would call each other witches secretly, and I even used the crystal ball emoji beside her name in my phone contacts list. A month and half after my accident I met her and boyfriend for dinner. Before I went out on my leave from work when I broke my ankle, I was giving Jamie readings during our lunch breaks. It was great practice for me as there was no judgment or expectations to get it right. Before she picked me up for dinner, she asked me if I would bring my angel cards. Of course, I would. Then she suggested, "Maybe we can do a reading for Andy?" Andy was her fiancé. At this time, I wasn't charging for readings. I just wanted to get better at it.

After we had eaten, I brought out my cards. I was a kind of nervous to do this in front of Andy. Most guys I knew were not particularly into the woo-woo and spiritual stuff. Or at least most guys I knew until then. We first did a reading for Jamie. Her question had to do with when she would get pregnant or if she would be able to get pregnant. I knew they had been trying for a short time to have a baby. I closed my eyes as I usually do when I began a reading and took a deep breath. I called in the angels to help guide Jamie with her concerns of being able to get pregnant. I began to shuffle the cards. Once I got the feeling to stop shuffling, I drew her cards.

I truly think I am the angels' vehicle to provide people with the messages they are seeking. Sometimes I can shuffle for a long time until I get that internal nudge to stop. When I do readings, I pull from the top of the deck. Some angel card readers take from the middle of the deck or take the card that is sticking out. I set the cards to face down, so the client doesn't get distracted by what's in front of them. I like them to focus on the messages at the moment and not look at the future cards. During this time, I was also still using the guidebook that came with the Angel Card decks to interpret them. I learned later in Doreen Virtue's Certified Angel Card Reader Course that this was a big "no-no" to do during client readings. But, for now, I wasn't charging any money, and my ego was telling me I needed the guidebook.

I pulled three cards for Jamie in this reading. We used the past, present, and future reading, where the first card was the past, the second card was the present, and the third card was the future. To be honest, I do not remember the first or the last card I pulled for Jamie. The card I remember was the present card, "Cleanse and Detoxify" from the Daily Guidance from your Angels Oracle Cards by Doreen Virtue. When this came up, I asked, "Are you sure you are not already pregnant?"

I let her know, as she was drinking a glass of wine, that she needed to act as if she was already pregnant and nourish her body as if a baby was already growing inside. We laughed about the wine. For this card, I didn't even look in the guidebook. I just knew. The actual card states, "With great love and respect, we ask you to detoxify your precious and sensitive body. At your request, we'll help you to develop life-affirming ways to deal with stress, as well as ease any sorrows at shedding your old ways. Give your cares, worries, and concerns to us and feel the beautiful grace of your newly purified body." Now this card states nothing of being pregnant. However, that was the message that I received strongly from the card. I put together what the card said, the glass of wine and I had an overwhelming feeling that she was pregnant already.

A week or so after the reading, Jamie let me know that she was eight weeks pregnant and was pregnant at the time of our reading. I felt validated. I know it seems very egotistical to feel that way, but my confidence had a lot of improving to do. Especially, if I was going to start charging for these readings. I learned later from Doreen Virtue that it was imperative to charge for readings or at least some kind of energy exchange. If I didn't do this, then I might feel unappreciated or not valued.

The reading for Jamie's boyfriend, Andy, was also pretty insightful. He asked about pursuing his writing career. I think he was concerned about whether he should get one of those "real" jobs, or go after his passion and continue his writing job, especially since he would be a Daddy soon! The card that I remembered for him was "Go for It" from the same deck that I used for Jamie. The card read, "Your Prayers and positive expectations have been heard and answered. We have been working with you on this situation since its genesis, and we continue to watch over you and everyone involved. Stay on your present path, as it will take you very far indeed." How encouraged Andy must have felt to hear this angel message. Andy continues to write full time, and he and Jamie are very happy with their little boy, James.

More and more readings were happening for me this way. I kept asking the angels to guide me and give me signs that this was my true path. I liked the feeling of being able to help people and to provide them reassurance that the angels had their back. I had learned that everyone has at least two guardian angels. I also learned that angels don't discriminate. They would help everyone, even if the person had done wrong in the past. All we need to do is ask.

Shortly after Jamie's reading, I met with a group of friends that were interested in receiving angel messages. One of my friend's friend asked about his job. He had been having a terrible time with a co-worker for years causing him to be sick inside when he was around them. This co-worker occupied more time in this guy's brain than necessary because it was only doing damage to him, not to the irritating co-worker. He asked specifically about his job and if he should leave. The future card pulled was, "Time to Go!" The Time to Go card from Doreen Virtue's Daily Guidance from the Angels says, "The sun sets and rises each day, and it's the same with the avenues in your life. See the beauty within each sunset of your life, and know that the sun will also rise again tomorrow. Endings are merely the start of a new beginning, and we are with you through each phase and cycle." This client said the card gave him chills, as he knew this was true for him. Comfort, familiarity, and his other work friends are what had been keeping him there.

I am not sure if he ever left, but it was up to him. Was he going to continue to allow this co-worker to live rent free in his head? Something I have learned through my spiritual growth is to no longer allow others to bring my spirit down. I was so affected by what others said and did, being an empath. It was very hard to shut down those emotions. I insisted on being the judge and putting everything on trial whether it was right or wrong. It only damaged me. The other individual usually went on their merry way with minimal harm, while I suffered because of my need to provide justice. My head is only rent-free to positivity and love today. That wasn't the case before I connected with my angels and spirit.

Doing readings for myself became a regular practice. I would ask the angels for guidance on virtually every aspect of my life. How to handle an awkward conversation? Will I ever get promoted at my job? Will I find the perfect apartment? Am I doing my life's purpose? Do I have a gift in doing angel card readings? I still asked that last question a lot, continuing to doubt myself even after having "spot on" readings. By doing readings on myself, it allowed me to get to know the cards and ditch the guidebook. The night before I was due back to my job from my ankle injury medical leave, I consulted my angels. I had a lot of anxiety about how things were going to be at work which I needed to release. Most of the problems there were because everyone, including myself, was gossiping and not confronting the person causing us stress with issues. I could only control my part in the situation. It was creating a lack of belief in myself and didn't make me excited to go to work.

I asked, "What do I need to know and focus upon with my team when I go back to work?"

I was worried about it because when I had left four months earlier, things were tough. I used Doreen Virtue's and Radleigh Valentine's Fairy Tarot deck and "Release" came up. This card could not have been any more perfect. The card states, "Let go of the past. An ending that makes way for new opportunities. Time to move on." Amen. I hadn't been there in four months. I am sure a lot had changed, and it was time for me to stop projecting into the future based on past actions. My angels were telling me to surrender and let go. I love when my teacher, Gabby Bernstein says, "When you think you have surrendered, surrender some more." I continued to surrender my fears and trust in my angel's guidance about my job and eventually the stressful situation resolved itself.

I have found that doing readings for family members has been challenging. I just seem not to be able to tap into their angels because of the family enmeshment. My ego gets in the way, and my third eye chakra is clogged and distracted. I want to tell them what I think they want to hear which I believe confuses the angels. I started to doubt myself when I would try to do readings for my mom and sister. I have since learned through the Hay House Certified Angel Card Reader Course (CACR) that this is normal. What a relief! Now, I don't even try to do a reading for my family as it lowers my energy. I will talk more about this fantastic CACR course in the next chapter.

Chapter 7
God Shot

"Believe in yourself. You have the power to heal and
manifest anything and everything."
-Doreen Virtue

About a month and a half after I broke my ankle I
was settling into myself. I had read, *Anatomy of the
Spirit* and *Defy Gravity* by Caroline Myss, *Wishes
Fulfilled* by the late Dr. Wayne Dyer and *Angels of
Abundance* and *Assertiveness for Earth Angels* by
Doreen Virtue. I was well on my way to the
individual I was meant to be. Good news, too, I was
able to get a scooter to get around a bit more. I was
no longer confined to my house! I could scoot to the
Target one block away, go out to eat at a few places
just three blocks away and go to the movies at the
Laemmle Theater. I had a sense a freedom that I
hadn't felt in the first six weeks of the accident. I
would spend hours a day sitting in the Starbucks at
Target, reading all these self-help books and
journaling what would now be thoughts for this
book. The team at Target was wonderfully helpful
and were sometimes the only people I talked to all
day. I had only been in Pasadena a little over a year
and hadn't found my tribe yet. Every time I came in
the Target team would always ask how my ankle was

and helped me find a table to sit where I could fit my scooter. I wasn't feeling so alone anymore. Their kindness and generosity was what got me through some of those days.

Jamie, who loaned me *Anatomy of the Spirit* and whose pregnancy I predicted, let me know that she was going to be in Pasadena at the Hay House "I Can Do It!" conference. At that time, I had no idea what Hay House was. I couldn't believe what I had been missing out on all these years! I went online to www.hayhouse.com to take a look at this event. I was quite excited to see that Doreen Virtue was going to be teaching her last in-person Certified Angel Card Reader Course. This course being her last in-person event in the city I live in, a few months after I had purchased my first deck of Angel Cards, was certainly a *God shot*. It was destiny, without a doubt! As much as I enjoyed Caroline Myss's book, I was drawn to Doreen Virtue. I still only had one deck of Doreen's Angel Cards. I had been doing readings for my friends that had been pretty "spot on," as they say, but I didn't feel confident doing them for strangers or charging money for readings. I was beyond grateful that I could hop on my scooter to get to the class. It was only eight blocks from where I lived! It was perfection, and I was thoroughly pumped about it. I was going to find my confidence. I just felt it!

I have to admit my expectations for the class were slightly off. I never imagined there would be such a big crowd! I thought there were going to be about 50-100 attendees; there were closer to 500 angel-loving people there. I believed I was going to sit at a table with THE Doreen Virtue and shoot the shit with her. I had no idea how influential she was up until this point. Initially, I was disappointed, but then I was amazed that there were so many people like me! People who believed in angels, and wanted to learn more from Doreen. I still can't believe that I had never heard of Doreen Virtue until I was 38 years old. I was a rather embarrassed about it. I felt all the people in this room had been studying her for years. I walked into the meeting hall and drank in all the energy in the room. Since I arrived pretty early, I found a spot about ten rows back. For the class, they were giving away a deck of Doreen's cards, so I sat in a chair that had The Angel Tarot deck by Doreen Virtue and Raleigh Valentine. Not knowing what the difference was between the smaller decks (Oracle cards) and bigger decks (Tarot cards), I chose this spot because I thought, the bigger, the better. That was such an ego move that I am laughing now. Tarot decks have 78 cards, and Oracle decks typically have 44 cards. To be honest with you I was a slightly intimidated by the Tarot Decks .... many more cards to learn and memorize! Maybe it wasn't my ego choosing that deck. Maybe it was spirit telling me *I Can Do It!*

I looked around the room becoming more and more overwhelmed with everyone running towards the front of the class to try to get as close as possible and to grab the decks of cards they wanted. People were leaving gifts for Doreen at her podium and hanging out up front in hopes of talking with her as she entered the stage. A lady sat next to me and was instantly very chatty. I was nervous as hell being around all these strangers, but once she began talking I realized I wasn't among strangers. I was with individuals like me. I am normally very shy around people I do not know and am not one to strike up a conversation with a stranger.

"I am so excited! I love Doreen; she is my idol! I need to meet her today," she let me know. I told her that I hadn't heard of Doreen until a few months before.

"No way! I have been using her cards for years," she said. She let me know she was a psychic and has been working with clients for a long time.

"Oh, I am pretty new at this. In fact, this is only

my second deck of cards, and I only have done readings for my friends." She seems shocked by this. Not because she thought I was lame for coming to this class not knowing what I was getting myself into, but because she believed in me. I felt it. She reminded me that she was going to talk with Doreen today and that she had come a long way. Myself, being the super people pleaser I was, wanted to support her in her dream to connect with Doreen. Therefore, every time Doreen solicited the audience to speak, I didn't raise my hand. I didn't want to be the one person to eliminate my classmate's dreams because I was selected to speak and she wasn't.

I was enlightened during the class. I learned so much about angels, oracle cards, tarot cards, angel numbers and how to create an angel card reading business. We practiced a lot of readings on each other, and I felt more and more comfortable as the day went on. It does take a lot of courage to give a reading to a complete stranger, who probably knows more about angels and angel cards than you. I was stoked! It was a boost to my ego, but in the right way, to be validated by my classmates that I could do this. Doreen gave plenty of opportunities for the audience members to speak with her and I noticed the lady next to me, whose mission was to meet Doreen, hadn't raised her hand once. Why, then, was I not raising mine? Just before lunch, Doreen introduced her angel posse who was helping her throughout the class. She mentioned specifically about writing a book with one of her angel friends on addiction recovery. She said if we had any stories to contribute to let her co-author know during the class. On the break, I approached this angel covered in glitter and sparkles about the book.

"Is there going to be anything infused in the book for friends and family of the alcoholic," I asked her? Since I was a grateful member of Alanon for nine years at the time, I thought I could offer my experience, strength, and hope. She said yes, and gave me her contact details. Sweet! The day was already pretty magical. I was on a spiritual high from all the positive vibes and genuine love in the room.

When we got back from lunch, Doreen started right off by asking if anyone in the class wanted a romance reading. She called one lady up to the front and asked her how the angels could help. The woman mentioned she was struggling in her current relationship and wanted to know if she should leave. Doreen told the lady something like, "You have a room of 500 people who are going to do a reading for you." Doreen then asked us all to pull three cards for the lady. I closed my eyes, centered myself and whispered in my mind for the angels to come into the reading to provide this woman with some sound loving messages. I could tell she was in pain, as she was crying. I pulled my three cards from my new Angel Tarot deck.

Doreen asked the audience, "Does anyone want to share their reading?" I looked at the girl next to me, and she still wasn't raising her hand to talk to Doreen. So, I raised mine. Seriously, I wanted to speak to this woman, Doreen, whom I found fascinating and was becoming obsessed with. What was I waiting for? With my hand raised I smiled as brightly as I could. Doreen asked her sparkly angel helper to bring me a mic. Oh shit.

"Hi, darling, what is your name?" Doreen asked me.

"My name is Tara," I said and simply smiled.

"Such a beautiful name, Tara." Doreen said my name was beautiful. I couldn't even focus. "What messages did you get from the cards?" I do not remember what I pulled for this woman, but it was something along the lines of her needing to move on and that she would be taken care of by her angels. It was pretty similar to Doreen's reading for her.

Doreen told the woman to find me after class that she felt I had more guidance to share. She also told me I did a great job! How wonderful to receive that validation from the most renowned angel card reader out there. I was smiling and full of love. My confidence was blooming by the minute.

"That is so awesome! I am happy for you." My new angel friend next to me said.

"Why haven't you raised your hand? I was hoping you would have a moment with Doreen." I asked her. She let me know she was feeling tired and really didn't have the energy. The rest of the day went by quickly. We learned about all the archangels, different kinds of angel card readings, how to start your angel card business and a lot more practicing of readings on my new friends. At the end of the day, Doreen was going to sign her cards and books. I only had the two decks of cards, so I would be quick. Other attendees had piles of stuff for her to sign. Since I was still in a cast on my scooter, I tried to get out of the ballroom hall as fast as possible to get in the line. I was about 100 people back. I saw my friend who sat next to me getting ready to leave.

"Wait. Are you leaving? I thought you wanted to meet Doreen." I asked her. Here I am again caretaking someone I just met because I wanted her to meet Doreen more than she wanted it for herself.

"I do, but I am so very tired, and I have to drive three hours home." She said. "But, I wanted to give you something. Your energy brought me up all day long, and you made me feel so warm. Your spirit is amazing. I hope you believe in your gifts after today." I started to cry. This was one of the kindest things someone had said to me at that point. She made crystal-wrapped jewelry and gave me a Selenite wrapped pendant. The crystal was very magical. I didn't know then, but Selenite helps to connect to the Divine light for personal transformation. Perfect. My life was about to be transformed.

"Thank you! That is one of the nicest things anyone has said to me. I love the pendant. Please stay in line with me. Come on. You came all this way to meet her. Don't go home now. Wait in line with me. The line is going fast." I convinced her. She stayed and had the opportunity to meet her longtime idol. I took their picture as Doreen was signing her deck of cards.

Then it was my turn. I was so nerdy when I got up to her. I was shy as usual and basically thanked her for a wonderful day and calling on me. She signed my two decks, and I went on my way. I have learned from living in Los Angeles and working retail not to linger too long with celebrities and invade their space. Just treat them like a regular human being. I know Doreen isn't a Hollywood celebrity like the ones I have met, but I wanted to respect her time and boundaries. I said goodbye to my friend and wished her the best. I hopped on my scooter to head home with my heart beaming brightly. I was a real certified Doreen Virtue Angel Card Reader. How wonderful is that?

My friend Jamie sent me a text to ask how my day was with Doreen and persuaded me to come the next day to listen to Caroline Myss and Brian Weiss speak. My financial fears told me to not spend the money, but I decided I was worth the investment. As the day started we were able to pick a few speakers we would like to see. Since I was a Hay House virgin and wasn't familiar with the speakers, I gravitated to anyone who had psychic or medium next to their name. I chose Brian Weiss, Caroline Myss and James Van Praagh. I loved James Van Praagh and his gift of speaking with crossed-over loved ones. Of course, like everyone else, I was hoping he would see a loved one of mine, specifically my Grandma Edith, who I mentioned earlier in the book. He called out to someone in the audience who had a black and white picture of a man folded in half in their wallet. He was very specific and asked that no one raise their hand unless this resonated with them. An older lady shyly raised her hand, and he called her up to the stage.

"Do you have the picture folded in your wallet?" He asked her. She answered him yes. "Can I see it?" She gave him the picture. "Yes, this is it." The man who had crossed over that James was seeing was this woman's deceased husband. She began crying and was so hysterically emotional. You could feel the love that she and her husband had for each other. It was overwhelming. I was bawling my eyes out. James asked the woman if she had two closets in her bedroom. The woman did.

"Your husband, Tom, but you called him Tommy, only you called him Tommy, Is that correct?" She answered him, "yes."

"He is telling me that he would like you to get the exercise equipment out of the closet on the right and start working out." She began laughing. It must have been an inside joke between the two of them. James Van Praagh also told her that he wanted her to know that Tommy never liked to carry her purse in public. James also told the lady that Tommy remembers her at his bedside when he was dying to tell him how much she loved him. He wanted his wife to know he loved her too.

I had never seen in real life a medium in action. I was amazed. The comfort James provided this woman was loving and kind. The rest of the day went on to be equally inspiring. I couldn't help but bounce through the day with a glow and feeling that I was touched by spirit. I met up with Jamie in the main lecture hall to listen to Brian Weiss. I found our seats and sat next to this woman with a strong accent. We talked about the conference, and I had told her about how awesome the Angel Card Reader class was.

"You do angel card readings?" she asked.

"Yes, would you like me to do one for you?" I offered because one of our assignments was to do a reading for a stranger. And because I do as I am told, I was eager to offer.

"Sure, I can pay you."

"Don't worry about it; it is good practice for me," I assured her. It did feel wonderful to be offered money for my work. The woman asked about her life in general. She was struggling and hadn't ever found her purpose. She wanted to know what the angels wanted to tell her. As I started to read her cards, she began to cry. I remember this woman's reading specifically because I wrote the cards down in my notebook. I used my favorite deck, Daily Guidance from the Angels by Doreen. The first card I pulled which signified the past, was "Family." The words on this card are truly beautiful. "This situation is rooted in an emotional experience with a family member, which we can help you to understand and heal. In your mind and heart, surround this person, yourself and the event with calming blue light and many angels. Be open to the gifts within the situation, and allow yourself to feel peace." The woman was crying as I interpreted this card for her because her father was killed in the country of her upbringing during a violent drug riot. She had held on to so many emotions from this situation, and it was holding her back.

The next card I pulled was "Heart Chakra," which represented the present. The card says, "Love is in the heart of the matter. Your heart is the center of your physical being attuned most to love. It's safe for you to love and be loved with an open heart, as we stand by with perfect protection and guidance." It was time for her to mourn the loss of her father and remove that grief and open up to receive love. She held my hands and continued to sob.

The final card, the future, was "Acceptance." This fit so perfectly with the "present" card as is says, "See yourself and others through the eyes of the angels, with unconditional love and acceptance. In this way, you inspire and lift everyone to their highest potential." This card was all about her practicing self-care and letting the past go. She thanked me for the reading and took pictures of each card. She was genuinely appreciative and moved by her angel's messages; it made me feel like I was in the right spot at the right time. Just as we finished our reading, Jamie came up. I introduced her to my new client. "Isn't she a gifted reader?" Jamie asked the woman. "She predicted my pregnancy." We all had chatted for a while before Brian Weiss took the stage.

I wasn't very familiar with Dr. Brian Weiss. I knew he did past life regressions, but that was it. I was excited that he was going to do a past life regression with us in the auditorium. All I knew about my past life was I had been told by a psychic I was reincarnated as my mom's sister, Janice who had passed when she was only five years old. I felt very strong this was true. If you aren't familiar with what a past life regression is, wikipedia.com says, "A past life regression is a technique that uses hypnosis to recover what practitioners believe are memories of past lives or incarnations." Most people know the book *Many Lives, Many Masters* by Dr. Brian Weiss. This book documents one of Brian Weiss's patients as she channeled messages from the "space between lives." He was able to help this client heal her recurring nightmares and anxiety attacks while at the same time uncovering some revelations about his son who had passed. If you haven't read it, I highly recommend it or listening to the audio book.

In this session, we got a taste of what a past life regression would look like. I have never encountered something so wild. I was able to see myself in a gypsy town and even heard the jingle of ankle bracelets with bells on them. I was dancing to the music being played by my husband. What did this all mean? I really would love to uncover this as I believe some of my old behaviors were inherited from my past life. My psychic, Ambika that I regularly see later confirmed my memories during my past life regression with Dr. Brian Weiss. Without me even discussing my experience with Dr. Weiss, I asked her about my past lives. She said I was a gypsy in a past life who gave psychic readings to the Kings in Romania. She told me the Kings would secretly come to me for advice. In exchange for my secrecy, my family was taken care of financially. She also said I had an alcoholic husband who was an accomplished musician and a daughter that had a voice of an angel. Dr. Brian Weiss and these past live regressions were absolutely fascinating to me. I had been exposed to so much in just one day, and Caroline Myss was up next!

Wow, this woman was intense! She was very direct and to the point and wasn't shy about speaking in hard truths. I liked her style. She said, "What I do to you, I do to me. I'll treat you with kindness and grace if it kills me. This keeps me powerful and healthy." I have a few pages full of Caroline Myss wisdom that she shared that day. I can relate to her directness. She encouraged us to think about why we do things? Why do we make the choices we do? She got me thinking about my wounds of my childhood and life in general. She said, "Wounds, you are not going to control me anymore. You are not going to speak through me anymore." I mentioned before about her book, *Anatomy of the Spirit*. The key take-away from her talk was to give up the need to know why things happen as they do. If I can let go of that need, I will no longer fall victim to my wounds. I can learn from them and move on with my life, no longer being held back. This same idea about old wounds was brought to my attention by my spiritual teacher, Gabby Bernstein. She says, "Your wounds are your wisdom." When you hear similar messages multiple times, I call it a "God shot." God, I hear you loud and clear.

I had to laugh when Caroline Myss said, "Your friends are sick of you complaining. Do you know how many of your friends are in therapy because of you?" I am sure there is some truth in her statement for my friends. In the past, I dumped on them often, which I am certain, sucked the life out of them. I feel sorry that I was that kind of friend back then. I am so grateful that my friendships today are more balanced and there is an equal giving and receiving. Caroline Myss emphatically said, "Start Over Today!" And, that I did. When I left the "I Can Do It" Conference I walked away feeling stronger, grounded, inspired and more confident. Doreen, James, Brian and Caroline motivated me. I was ready to embrace more of who I was and stand tall in my fresh spiritual start. Let's do this.

Chapter 8
Making an Amends

*"Those who are free of resentful thoughts
surely find peace."*
-Buddha

Now that I had all this spiritual *mojo* and the
angels on my side, it was time to head Phoenix,
Arizona, to get Chester back and have a serious
conversation with my mom. I needed to ask for
forgiveness for the way I acted on the beach and
back at my apartment. Apologizing is so hard. Have
you ever had to make amends to someone first, from
whom you had been waiting for an apology your
whole life? My mom did apologize after the accident
for my feelings of being the adult and her the child,
but not for anything specific. I have learned to
accept that this is where she is today. I don't get to
decide and create the apology for her. She redeemed
herself the best way she knew how. The opportunity
that I have is to forgive her. This quote by Dr. Wayne
Dyer sums up this position I was in:

"You practice forgiveness for two reasons: to let
others know that you no longer wish to be in a state
of hostility with them and to free yourself from the
self-defeating energy of resentment. Send love in

some form to those you feel have wronged you and notice how much better you feel."

I was nervous about getting to the airport, going through airport security and flying on the plane with my broken ankle and my scooter. It probably was too soon to be getting my boy back, but I missed him so much. I prayed to my angels to get me through this trip and to help me with Chester when I got back home. Airport security was super fun. The hardware in my ankle was for sure going to set off some alarms. This whole situation tested my capability to ask for help. Asking for help from others is not one of my strengths. I saw this as a universal assignment. I asked complete strangers for help with my luggage, to get to the restroom, to help with my scooter down the ramp to the aircraft, to get down the aisle of the airplane and to put my bag in the overhead compartment. All things I would have rather died over than ask for help before. I know, a little dramatic. This ankle accident was bringing me to my knees. Thank you, spirit. I gave myself an A+ for that spiritual assignment.

My mom was so kind and brought Chester with her to the airport. Oh man, I bawled like the biggest baby when I saw him. He was really jazzed to see me, jumping about and whimpering and kissing me.

Such love, he and I had for each other. It was like he didn't even remember that his mommy left him for six weeks. A dog's love is always unconditional. It is refreshing to see how quickly they forget and move on. I was equally excited to see my mom and give her a long hug too.

"I love you, Mom," I whispered in her ear while holding her tightly. I adjusted myself into the back seat as my mom's boyfriend folded down my scooter into the trunk. I was still wearing my air cast which was clunky and quite frankly, unfashionable! I wasn't allowed to bear weight on it yet. You don't realize how valuable your feet are until you aren't able to use them. They carry all of your weight all day long. As my dad told me, "You only have two feet, and you can't walk on your hands." My Dad is a joker, but he was absolutely right. I learned the hard way having to have additional foot surgeries after I broke my ankle. "Be kind to your feet," another universal lesson from this accident.

I also wasn't driving yet. Having to rely on rides everywhere or taking public transportation was also an opportunity to grow. This was the first time being in Arizona for a visit where I couldn't just take off to see and go where I wanted. There are millions of people all over who do not have the means to have a vehicle or who take public transportation every day. My sister is one of them. She rides her bike everywhere even though sometimes it's over 100-degree temperatures in Phoenix, Arizona. Having to take public transportation on a scooter was stressful, but I was deeply moved by the complete strangers who were so helpful to me. I am grateful now to public transportation because it gave me the ability to get out of my apartment and enjoy the beautiful city where I was blessed to live while I was recovering and unable to drive. Today, even though I can drive, I still enjoy taking the Metro Gold Line in Pasadena! It can get you into downtown Los Angeles in only 30 minutes, much quicker than driving in traffic.

Back to my return trip home. It felt awesome, to be in Arizona, with my Mom and Chester and to just relax and enjoy her company in a space where I wasn't so freaked out, scared of what's next, and trying to figure out what to do. I think they call this control, the need to know what is happening at any given moment. However, on this day I was at a place of surrender. I could stay present because there was nothing for me to do, but enjoy my family. Plus, I had an amends to make. My first amends ever in my nine years of Alanon, even though I wasn't on Step Eight yet in my Alanon program, "Make a list of all persons we had harmed, and became willing to make amends to them all." I have learned that I can always admit guilt for my wrong behavior whether I am at Step Eight or not. I want to be clear, I have apologized to people in the past, but this time I needed to work through it with a mentor and my friends. I journaled about it, and I turned the outcome over to my Higher Power by placing it into my Angel Box. Before when I apologized, I had expectations on the outcome. And although at the time I felt my atonement was authentic, I see now that if I am saying sorry with expectations, it wasn't coming from a place of complete truth.

I had planned a day with my mom to hang out. We were going to the movies and coffee. I have to admit I was nervous. I reminded myself that the apology a part of my healing work. Her reaction to my amends had nothing to do with me. It was going to help me to forgive myself for my behavior at the beach and release the energy that was blocking me. I wasn't proud of the way acted towards her. I was really embarrassed. At Vroman's Bookstore, I had found her a little stone that had the word "Grace" on it, because that is exactly how she handled things, with grace. We sat down at the coffee shop, and I could feel my heart pounding. I was about to get real and vulnerable with my mom, where in the past I had a hard time expressing how I felt with her.

"Mom, I have something I want to talk to you about." I started off.

"What's wrong?" She asked that because tears were already welling up in my eyes.

"I am ashamed of the way I treated you on the beach and back at my apartment. I was awful to you. The way I yelled and screamed at you was horrible."

"You were scared. I have never seen you so freaked out." She was trying to make me feel better.

"Nothing like that has ever happened to me. I was completely freaked out. But it wasn't an excuse to treat you like crap. I took my anger out on you and all the resentment from years where I felt I took care of you, just came out."

"I didn't realize you felt that way. I am sorry." She said.

"I have done so much for you over the years; I always felt there was an imbalance in our relationship. I wanted you to do something on the beach and take care of it, make it go away. I wasn't even listening to anything you suggested. I am sorry, Mom. I love you so much. And I am extremely proud of you being sober." I cried deeply as the words came out of my mouth. It still brings a deep emotion out of me today.

"I got you something." I pulled out the 'Grace' stone and gave it to her. "You handled everything with such grace on the beach when I screamed at you and when I tried to kick you out of my apartment the night before the surgery. When you grabbed my hand in my room and reminded me that you were my mother and that you loved me, I will never forget that moment. I thought this small stone was perfect." By this time, we were both crying. Sometimes it can be hard to cry openly with such emotion in a public place, but my mom and I didn't let that sensor our tears. Having compassion for my mother is what ultimately got me to a place of forgiveness with her. I leaned over to give her a hug, "I love you, Mom."

It was my angels and the Divine stepping into my life when that accident happened with my mom. As close as my mom and I have always been over the years, and no matter how much love I had for her, there was serious work to be done in our relationship. I was always going to hold on to those resentments against her and have anger and low vibrational energy with her until I could get to a place of forgiveness. This was the first step towards our recovery together in having a healthy Mother/Daughter relationship. I was happy and relieved after that conversation. I felt good, and so did she. Things changed with my mom after I made my amends. We grew closer, which I wouldn't have thought we could be any closer than we already were. Today, we are healthy, closer and less enmeshed than before. Not to say that old behaviors don't pop up with my mom and me. In fact, they just did this week. But, today we can talk about it and say how we made each other feel without worrying if it would upset each other.

Not only was this trip home therapeutic for my mom's and my relationship, but my dad and I were able to spend some time together, too. Since I couldn't drive, he had to drive out to my mom's house to pick me up for a road trip to Flagstaff to see some of my family. I mentioned a bit in the first chapter about my dad. My mom and my dad divorced before I was born, so I really didn't have a connection with him when I was a child. I remember visiting him twice a week when I was little. But, those visits stopped when he moved to California. I don't even remember how old I was at that time, maybe nine. When he was in California, my siblings and I flew out there once a year in the summer for a week's visit. It was always a lot fun because we got to go to the beach and Disneyland. Not that my Dad was a Disneyland Dad, but we did get to do a lot more things with him because money didn't seem to be an issue as it was for my mom. We had family dinners and played board games; it felt safe to be there. I knew my mom and he did not really like each other, fought often and went to court over child support a few times during my childhood. I don't think my dad realized how much my mom struggled with raising us kids with the income she made and the child support he provided. My siblings were not a walk in the park and put my mom through a lot. I always felt I was in the middle of my parent's anger and resentment with each other. I was with my mom the majority of the time and was her protector and defender, so I developed resentments with my dad too. I felt he wasn't there. He usually never came to my softball games or jazz band concerts. He really didn't know what was going on with us. When he moved back to Arizona, the weekly visits with him never resumed. I intermittently saw my dad in my late teen years through my early 30's. When I was in town, he never knew it. I didn't receive birthday or Christmas cards from him. I was hurt. The one male relationship where every woman should learn about trust, love, and men was void for me. I know this deficiency in a Father and Daughter connection, has contributed to my lack of trust in men.

Before my biological brother, who is just one year older than me, was deployed to Iraq, my dad came back into the picture. It was super awkward for me. I continued protecting my mom and making sure she was okay when we would all be in the same room together. I had nothing in common with my dad. I knew nothing about him and him nothing about me. At least my biological brother and he could talk about cars, fixing things and hunting. They even went on a trip to Alaska together. At that time if I knew I was going to go on a trip with my dad with just the two of us, I would have strangled myself with anxiety. Today, I can say this is not the case for me. Although we did not go to Alaska, we have taken several road trips to Flagstaff to see my half-brother, sister in law and youngest niece.

It's such a beautiful thing to get to know your father and share a little about yourself with him. Although my dad doesn't know much about my spiritual ways, I feel completely comfortable and safe spending time with him and sharing some of the things going on in my life. We have a common interest in animals, especially dogs. We could talk about dogs forever. I am grateful today for my relationship with my dad, and because I took a leap of faith to forgive him and show him that I could make time for him, as well as for my mom when I come to town. By me having faith, it is helping me with my trust in male relationships and friendships.

Chapter 9
I Found My Tribe

"Surround yourself with only people who are going to lift you higher."
-Oprah Winfrey

I had no idea there were so many angel-loving light workers in this beautiful world until I started to find my tribe. I thought that I was the only one with these crazy ideas in my head about angels and trusting in the Universe. When I was taking my Certified Angel Card Reader Course CACR in October 2014, I saw an ad flash on the screen about Doreen coming to Orange County to teach her Certified Angel Intuitive Course the following October. I knew I was going. The decision to go was incredibly easy! I wasn't sure where the money would come from, but my soul knew I would get there. I was right, I set the intention that I wanted to go, and I envisioned myself there with Doreen. I paid for the course almost ten months early which made it extra hard to wait ten months! In Chapter 11 I write more about my manifesting skill and how I have been able to manifest abundance with perfect timing.

The Angel Intuitive Course is a three-day class

surrounded by light workers, angel lovers, mediums, clairvoyants, psychics and just all-around loving beings with the highest vibrational energy from all over the world! This course was one of the most special weekends of my life because I learned I was not alone. The energy in the room was both magnetic and uplifting that I felt like I was on a cloud as soon as I walked in the doors. I was greeted by smiles with pure light behind the eyes of the person smiling. I got there early each day because I wanted to sit as close to the front as possible. I was getting more and more nervous as the registrants flooded the room on the first day. I was a closeted introvert. Friends always thought I was outgoing and class clown of sorts. But I often faked it until I made it. I was good at that. However, crowds of people that I didn't know scared me. Crowds equaled a lot of energy that affected me in minutes. Since attending the CACR course and reading more self-help books by my new spiritual teachers, I learned that I was an empath. It really explained a lot about me, as I was always sensitive to others' emotions. I am not sure if this is something I learned while growing up or if I was born this way. I would get super upset watching Lifetime movies and Hallmark commercials because, even though I wasn't able to feel my own emotions during my childhood, I could feel the emotions of others. On the second and third day, I did not have that apprehensive feeling that was there the first day. What a true testament to the collective positive energy of acceptance, love, and light in that room and the tribe of individuals that Doreen had gathered.

Two lovely ladies sat next to me, one of them had the warmest smile I had ever seen. Her name was Catherine, and she lives in Sedona, Arizona, and owns a crystal shop named Follow your Heart. I have since visited her shop, and we stay in contact, supporting each other in our aspirations. We even ran into each other at a Gabby Bernstein event in Arizona in October 2016 without knowing each other was going to attend. These women embraced me, and I felt at ease pretty quickly in their presence. We enjoyed each other so much on the first day that we decided to sit together the next few days. The weekend was magical. I felt I was at Angel Camp where we sat on cotton candy clouds and rode unicorns all day. I was flying high into my crown chakra, which was my favorite chakra to live. We learned all about angel card reading, realm reading, aura readings, mediumship, Doreen even talked about book publishing and Radleigh Valentine talked about social media with Robert Reeves. We were given the opportunity to partner with others, to practice all these magical modalities. And, I was paid

for my first reading! My confidence was soaring, and
when Angel Camp ended, I knew I could do
anything I set my mind too.

When Doreen talked about publishing a book,
this is where I zeroed into every word she was saying.
She talked about how she started with Hay House
and back then you didn't need to have an agent. I
was fascinated. I could listen to her talk about books
all day. I knew then that I was going to write a
memoir and it was going to be published by Hay
House. She alerted us that things had changed since
she published her first book and that for one to be
published, they must have a platform and a social
media following, both of which I didn't have. Luckily
for me, Radleigh and Robert were up next to talk
about social media and platforms. One of the first
things, Radleigh said was to try to write for smaller
publications first. He said he wrote for a UK based
magazine called *Soul & Spirit Magazine*. He
mentioned that most likely we wouldn't get paid for
what we wrote, but it would help us build our
platforms.

The next day when I got home, I got busy! I
opened my Instagram account as
@serenity_of_the_angels and used the picture of
Doreen and me from the angel party we had during

"Angel Camp." I put my marketing skills to work and felt people would trust me as an angel card reader if I had a picture of myself with Doreen. My first post was on October 14, 2015, and it was a meme I made that said, "Surrender Is Not Submission" which I took from my Alanon literature. It received 44 likes, which is angel numbers means "The Angels are giving you extra comfort, love, and support right now. Ask them for help with everything, and listen to their guidance through your intuition." (from Doreen Virtue's www.angeltherapy.com)

Today as I am writing this 15 months later, I have posted 1264 times and now I my account is @taraladue with a picture of me. Sure, I have a lot of followers compared to most, but Instagram became much more than just building my platform. I found my tribe, my serenity tribe. It makes me a little emotional to talk about because finding my tribe has been vital to my self-acceptance, success and recovery from childhood trauma. You have likely seen the hashtag flying around the internet #YourVibeAttractsYourTribe, and it is true. For me when I got on Instagram, I started to become my authentic self. I posted whatever woo-woo stuff I wanted, because I felt safe there with virtual strangers! None of my family or friends who know the old me were there to criticize or judge. With each post, I met more and more earth angels and light workers. I couldn't believe I was meeting "friends" on the internet. What would I tell my real-life friends about these things that were happening? I didn't tell them anything then because I assumed they would judge me. But, once I did, they didn't judge me at all.

Once I started building my platform, growing a tribe who accepted me for who I was, I began to advertise my angel card readings. I had built trust through my posts and, of course, having the two certificates from Doreen Virtue always helps. I began doing readings for clients throughout the world. For the first time, I felt really wonderful about myself. As my confidence grew, I remembered what Radleigh had told us about writing for smaller publications for free to get our writing and name out there. I decided to go big or go home. After setting the intention to write for *Soul & Spirit Magazine*, I contacted them and asked if I could write an article about angels. I let them know I had recently completed Doreen Virtue's Angel Intuitive course and Radleigh encouraged us to reach out to publications to write. I actually said, "I decided to go big or go home." Someone responded to me within a day, and this woman became my editor. She told me that I had really inspired her to take a leap of faith and just go for it. I wrote three articles for their online publications and contributed to their April 2016, and July 2016, hardcopy issues. Writing for this magazine gave me credibility and the nudge to start my own blog. I called it the Angel Love Blog, and then changed it to something simpler, "Angel Blog." You can read it here: www.taraladue.com/angelblog. I don't always write about angels every time, but you can count on inspiration and light when you read it, and that's a promise! Sadly, my editor left *Soul & Spirit Magazine*, and I have had zero success contacting anyone at the magazine since.

After a few months on social media, I became even closer to certain people whom I'd found online. If I had not listened to Doreen's advice about getting on social media, I wouldn't have the tribe I have today. I have built lifelong bonds with these soul sisters and brothers. They are my family. I have even had the opportunity to meet a few of these awe-inspiring "family members" in person, one being my dear friend, Carrie. Carrie and I had exchanged phone numbers and had only texted in the beginning. I just couldn't get over the idea of calling someone I only knew through Instagram. One day I really needed some advice about a client. I knew Carrie would be the perfect one to call, but my ego kept telling me, "You'd bother her if you called, and besides you can't call her, she doesn't even know you." But, she did know me. She knew exactly who I was. Carrie is a really talented medium and a very special earth angel. I know we knew each other in a past life. I finally picked up the phone and began to dial. My heart was beating so fast. I kind of hoped she wouldn't pick up and I could simply leave a voicemail.

"Hey, girl! I am glad you called." She was excited I called! She immediately made me feel comfortable

and as if I were in a warm embrace. I knew we were
going to be the sisters from another mister. We
talked forever! We had so much in common. We
were the same age. We both had Virgo rising in our
Astrology charts. We both grew up in alcoholism,
and we both experienced the same childhood
trauma. I could tell her anything! She helped me
with this client, as I knew she would, and we've
continued to talk often ever since. She even came to
visit me in Pasadena! We had a blast! We solidified
the past life bond we knew we had. People come
into your life for a reason, and I knew Carrie came
into mine to help me have confidence in myself to
walk through my childhood trauma. I am eternally
grateful that we "followed" each other on social
media, and very, very thankful. I also have to add
how interesting it is to be friends with a medium.
She can get a "download" at any time and start
sharing it with you in a phone call or text. I often get
texts from her saying, "Girl, I am really feeling your
heart today." I love getting those text messages.

Another very special lady I met was Mrs. Chayla
Baer. This girl, we could talk for hours, and she says
it exactly as it is. She says it this way because she
cares. She has been my number one supporter and
even asked me early on before we became friends to
write a guest blog on her website. I felt honored that

she saw something through my posts to invite me to share space on her blog. She believed in me and still does today. I can fall out of my light worker ways, and she loves me anyway. Chayla was so kind to read my book proposal before I sent it to Hay House. I trusted her to read it and knew she'd correct all my grammatical errors with love, as grammar is not one of my strengths. She gives me sound advice, and I trust her with all of my creative expressions. If I need someone to set me straight, Chayla is my girl. I thank my angels and Doreen often for pointing me to the place where I would meet soul sisters like Carrie and Chayla; they are just two of the love-filled people I have met who support me, guide me and encourage me to stand in my light, share my story, and write my book. Thank you, Carrie, Chayla and everyone else. I love you.

Through building my platform for this book, I fell in love with social media. During Carrie's visit, I did an interview for a successful social media consultant about authenticity on social media. She said to me a during the interview, "You are better at this than I am." By this, she meant growing a social media following from nothing with authenticity and integrity. When the interview was over Carrie said, "Why aren't you charging a fee for this?"

"For what?" I asked.

"Social media advice." She said it so confidently as if she truly thought I could help people. Maybe she was right. I was already handling social media for my Kundalini Yoga Studio in Pasadena, The Awareness Center.

Folks had been asking me for months, "How have you grown your social media following so quickly? How do you make those beautiful inspirational memes? What apps do you use?" I answered them because I wanted to help others. I wanted them to find what I found through social media. I hoped for everyone to find their tribe.

After I consulted my angels and put the idea in my Angel Box, I received the guidance to go for it! I sent an email out the next day announcing my social media coaching business. I posted it on all my social media platforms, and I waited. It was a big deal put myself out there. What if no one wanted to hire me? I had ten new clients in the first week! Most of the clients came from my Instagram following, which felt so good to see people believe in what I was posting online. They had watched my account evolve since day one. My tribe had seen me post with authenticity, love, and light when I had no previous following. No one knew who Tara LaDue was before I got on social media. My social media accounts spoke for themselves and to have this instant success validated that I was on the right path.

Once I started coaching people I knew I'd found my life purpose, to help spiritual entrepreneurs with their social media. Doing this form of teaching lit me up, and I felt fulfilled! The reviews started to come in as I booked more coaching clients. I even picked up a few more monthly retainer clients. I was able to go part-time with the job that allowed me to transition to my life purpose as a writer, Social Media Coach, and Angel Card Reader.

By the way, as you are transitioning into your life's work, it is so important to show gratitude to the job that has been paying you and affording you the means to do what you love. If it were not for my employer of seven years, all of these miracles wouldn't have unfolded for me. I feel very strongly that by the time you are reading this soul project of mine, I will have completely transitioned into my own life's work working very little the company that scared about me for so long. I believe this because I trust in my Higher Power and my angels.

Chapter 10
Signs From Above

"Yes, the signs you have been receiving are heaven-sent. We drop feathers, coins and other signs upon your path to remind you that you're loved and never alone."
-from "Notice the Signs"
Daily Guidance from your
Angels Oracle Cards by Doreen Virtue

I am now confident my angels have been speaking to me since I was born. I just wasn't ready to see, hear and smell the signs until my spiritual awakening back in September 2014, when I broke my ankle on Broad Beach in Malibu, California. When I look through some of my old belongings of angel knick-knack stuff from way before my spiritual awakening, it doesn't surprise me. Signs from your angels can come in so many forms. Coins, feathers, numbers, songs on the radio, words on a sign or even a butterfly following you on a walk. I often see my angel numbers on store receipts totals, and it just makes me smile every time! I have learned that I can even ask for signs. I often like to play around with my angels while I am practicing Kundalini Yoga. Often in Kundalini Yoga, we are asked to focus on our third eye point. During the Gong Meditation, I will ask my angels to show me certain colors in my

Third Eye Chakra. The Third Eye Chakra is the sixth Chakra and is indicated by the color indigo. According to the Chopra Center, an open sixth chakra, your "Sixth Sense," can enable clairvoyance, telepathy, lucid dreaming, expanded imagination, and visualization. The colors dance in my head like the Electric Light Parade at Disneyland. These colors, for me, usually tell me which of the Archangels are with me.

The most significant angel sign I can remember was one I received in a Lululemon shopping bag! I grabbed the bag to pack Chester's food, treats, and medicine for a stay with my cousin. When I opened the bag, there was a fortune inside of it. Why would a fortune cookie fortune be inside of this bag? I had never been to a Chinese restaurant with this bag. I pulled the fortune out of the bag, and it read, "Your charms have not gone unnoticed by all the angels." In the lucky numbers, 11 was the first number listed. I had seen versions of 11 ever since my ankle accident. It started off with 911, then 111 and 1111. 911 from www.angeltherapy.com means "It's very important that you keep a positive mindset concerning your spiritually-based career ideas. Positive thoughts are your most significant asset right now." I laugh when I remember myself first becoming a spiritual entrepreneur, because this was the first angel number I would see everywhere! 11 in Angel Numbers means "Stay positive! Your thoughts are materializing rapidly, so you want to ensure positive outcomes by focusing only on the good within yourself, others, and this situation." (from Doreen Virtue's *Angel Number's 101*) These numbers come to me on a clock, house numbers, zip codes, and even as I am scrolling through my Instagram newsfeed, I will see a post that has 11 or 111 likes.

Before I got into all this angel stuff, I moved to Pasadena in 2014. Is it odd that my zip code in Pasadena begins with 911? I think not. This was another sign from my angels that I made the right decision to move to Pasadena. 911 often shows up while driving. I will look to my right or left and see 911 or 111 as an address on a house or a business. I see it on license plates and people's Driver's Licenses. In fact, I helped someone the other day at my part time job who on their Driver's License showed part of their license number having 911 in it, their address was 11 and their zip code was 911 and their birthday was November 11th! I asked him, "Are you aware of what the number 11 means?" He had no clue. But when I explained to him he couldn't stop smiling and saying, "get out!" His wife came into meet him, and that was the first thing he told her.

One of the most interesting places I have experienced angel numbers is at the hospital or doctor's office! During my first hammer toe surgery, I was rolled into room 11 at a surgical center in Pasadena. I was beyond excited! I made my mom take a picture of it! Then almost one year later, before going into my reconstruction hammer toe surgery, I was put in bed 11 at the surgery center in San Gabriel. See the number 11 happens so often now that I just laugh. It makes me feel protected when my angels are around me showing me loving signs. A few months ago, at the dermatologist office, I noticed I was put in room 11. I asked my doctor, "Are you always in this room?"

She said, "Yes, why?" I smiled and told her to Google Angel number 11. When I went back to see my dermatologist, she said, "Hey! I Googled Angel number 11!"

"Oh, you did?" I had almost forgotten about the last visit!

"How awesome! I love it." She said. She went on to tell me that she was starting to notice other signs too.

I once saw a cop who had a police car numbered 44. I asked him, "Have you ever had a crazy accident or a scary incident on duty where you felt you were in danger?" He looked at me like I was an alien. He said, "no, why?" I then asked him, "Is that car number assigned to you or do you pick it every day?" He said he picks it every day because 44 is his lucky number. I told him to Google what number 44 means in angel numbers. "The angels are giving you extra comfort, love, and support right now. Ask them for help with everything, and listen to their guidance through your intuition." (from www.angeltherapy.com) He was blown away. He couldn't stop smiling, so pleased with himself about his lucky number cop car. He admitted he never believed in this kind of stuff before and acknowledged that I might be on to something. I responded, "You might be more spiritual than you think."

One of my favorite Angel signs happened in October of 2016. I was walking Chester after having my second round of Hammer Toe Surgeries on both feet. It was a struggle for me to get around. I looked down at my ring and noticed the main diamond missing. I was so upset! This ring was very special to me. A few Christmas's prior my mom didn't have much money for presents. She gifted me this ring that was my grandma Edith's. The diamonds had come out of her wedding ring with my grandfather and she designed this ring, putting those diamonds in it. I cried! I said out loud, "Archangel Chamuel, Grandma, where is this diamond?" How would I find this diamond? If anyone could help is was Archangel Chamuel, as he helps locate lost items. I could barely walk, and I had no clue where it would have fallen out. As soon as I got into my apartment, I heard my angels say, "Bathtub." I had just taken a shower. I got on my knees and looked all over in the tub and couldn't find it. I asked Archangel Chamuel, "Where in the bathtub?" I heard, "The bar soap." I pushed myself back up and looked in the bar of soap. There it was! I pulled it out and was amazed! At this point in my life, I had been hearing and feeling Angels for a few years, but this was really crazy! What is even more special is when I went to the jewelry store to have it fixed, I realized that losing the diamond was a message from my grandma. I had been wearing her ring on my wedding finger, almost as a protection from men, saying loud and clear, "I am unavailable." I decided while fixing the diamond to resize the ring to make my wedding finger available sending out the vibes that I am open to love.

My grandma is always with me. I wrote before about how much I love my grandma. I miss her so much, but she is never far away. She comes to me in the form of birds. When I am walking Chester, she

always finds me. I wonder if it is because I named my sweet Shih Tzu, Chester Harold after my grandfather, my grandmother's husband. I will ask the bird, "Grandma, is that you?" When I ask, I instantly feel the tears, and intense emotion builds under my eyes. It is such a heightened sensation that I feel behind and under my eyes, that tears usually build up. Never underestimate the power of your emotions. Those can be a sign that someone from the Divine or who has crossed over is near you. The birds are all around me now, chirping and buzzing and I usually say, "Hello, Grandma. I am grateful I have this connection with you."

An angel message came to me in the form of a Madonna song at the end of 2016, as I was driving home from spending time with my family for Christmas. My medical leave was ending in a few weeks after having the reconstructive Hammer Toe Surgery and being out of work for almost a year and a half. My life had completely transformed in that amount of time. My goals changed, my passions changed, and I loved what I was doing. I was a bit fearful of the next step I wanted to take, which was to go part time at the job that was allowing me to transition into my life's purpose. All sorts of old limiting financial beliefs crept in, and my ego was telling me, "No, No, you cannot do it." As I was leaving Blythe, California, I asked my angels to play me Madonna's "Rebel Heart," on my iPhone if it was meant for me to transition part-time and to know that I will be fully supported. I had my music on shuffle with over 20,000 songs. I kid you not, that song came on next! I completely questioned it. So, I asked again, "Play me Rebel Heart again, one more time before I pull off to go home." I had about 2 hours left until I made it back home. Rebel Heart didn't play again until I pulled off my freeway exit to get to my house. I love the lyrics in this song. The chorus sings, "So I took the road less traveled by. And I barely made it out alive. Through the darkness somehow I survived. Tough love, I knew it from the start. Deep down in the depth of my rebel heart." I wish I could say that I no longer question my angels when asking for and receiving signs, but I still ask for second and third confirmations.

Dr. Wayne Dyer is often with me exactly when I need him and usually when it has to do with this Memoir. When I finally went to Maui in August 2016, after changing my ticket a few times, I had my closest encounters with Wayne. On the plane ride there I made it my mission to tackle the most emotionally triggering and powerful chapter of this book, Chapter 13. I asked Wayne if he could help me have the courage and the strength to put my pain to paper. The words dripped out of me so easily, and I was able to write that chapter with ease and grace. When I landed, I looked at Instagram, of course, and saw that I had landed in Maui, Dr. Wayne Dyer's home city on the one-year anniversary of his death. Chills went up and down my spine. I had no idea this would happen and hadn't realized it had already been one year since his death. I was meant to go to Maui in June, then I had changed it to October and at the last minute decided to fly there on August 29, 2016, the one year anniversary of Dr. Wayne Dyer's death.

That wasn't the only time Wayne visited me on this trip. I felt him everywhere. On the following day, I decided to walk along the shoreline to Kahului Beach. I came across some rough rocky area and felt somewhat scared that I would injure my feet further. I was the only one out there, along with tons of crabs popping their heads out of the sand seeing who it was vibrating their dwellings. I closed my eyes and prayed for spirit and my angels to guide me to a magical spot. I stopped where some local fishers were casting their rods, dropped my backpack and simply stared into the ocean. The water was greenish blue; I had never seen anything like it. The sand sparkled. I sat down and pulled out my crystals and Doreen Virtue's Magical Mermaids and Dolphins Cards, the perfect deck to bring with me on my first trip to Hawaii.

I breathed deeply and thought of Wayne again. I must be honest; I am a bit of a Dr. Wayne Dyer

newbie only discovering him just a few years ago. I
have read about five of his books, and his messages
and teachings resonate with me. I asked him, "I
know you are with me, Wayne. I can feel you here so
strongly. What do you want to tell me?" I shuffled
my cards, and one card flew out with the wind as if
whispering to me. I am getting chills writing about
it. Alchemy was the card. This card validated to

keep putting my energy and light into my dreams.
Everything I have been manifesting since October
2015, will turn to gold. If you all knew what I have
been doing to realize my hopes, all the intentional
things I do, you might think I'm crazy! See chapter
11, Manifesting Queen! This card was perfection and

a gift. My angels always guide me in the right direction and tell me what I need to know at the perfect time.

On January 1, 2017, I did my annual angel card reading using the same deck I used in Maui, the Magical Mermaids and Dolphins Oracle Cards, along with the Guardian Angel Tarot deck. I thought as I shuffled the cards, I wonder if Wayne will show me the Alchemy card again. I asked, "Wayne if you are here, please show me the 'alchemy card.'" I got all the way to November 2017, and the card didn't come up in my reading. Then when I picked for December 2017, the 'alchemy card' came up. Pulling that card made me smile so big! I said out loud, "Wayne, I cannot wait to see what you have for me in December 2017!"

Just last month, I decided to scope out the location of where I broke my ankle. I thought it would be the perfect spot for the cover photo of this book! While I was there, I sat down in the sand where I had laid in complete pain when I fell and broke my ankle. I sat there in my clothes letting the salt water wash over me. I had the Magical Mermaids and Dolphins Oracle Cards deck in my hands and began praying. I asked, "Are you here, Wayne?" I took a deep breath in, and my body shuddered. The first card I pulled was "Alchemy." The exact message on this card is "You have the Midas touch right now, and every project you begin turns to gold." I took this as a miracle. All the reasons and significance of that exact spot on the beach, I knew he was telling me that I needed to publish this book.

Never underestimate the validity and magic of angel messages. My angels have saved me in some dangerous situations and helped me make crucial life decisions. Sometimes I don't even need anything major happening in my life, and they show me that they are right there sending me angel blessings. Angels are everywhere. I hope after reading this chapter that you will pay closer attention or maybe even ask for some signs from your angels. They want to communicate with you. They want to help guide you on your path. You can call on them anytime you need them. Never feel like they are too busy to help you. As Doreen Virtue once said, "You have powerful and loving Angels with you right now!"

Chapter 11
Manifesting Queen

*"What you think. And what you feel. And what
manifests is always a match.
Every single time. No exception."*
-Esther Hicks

It is no surprise that the chapter about
manifesting is Chapter 11, based on the last chapter
you read, that mentioned the significance of Angel
number 11. If I had known that when I aligned my
thoughts and actions to what I want out of my life,
the Universe would provide, I would have started this
thing called manifesting long ago! The term
"manifesting" didn't enter my soul until about two
years ago when the world changed for me, as we've
discussed so much already in this book. When I
think back on my life, I realize now I had been
manifesting stuff all along; I just didn't realize that
was what I was doing. I remember wanting to go
away to college in California, but I knew it would be
a stretch financially. I didn't have financial support
from my parents to go, and I would need to make it
happen all on my own. I prayed to whoever I prayed
to at the time, and I was accepted to a college in
California. The miracle was, I later learned, that
whoever entered in my application documents

registered that I went to Glendale Community College in Glendale, California, and not Glendale, Arizona, resulting in me paying instate tuition! That tiny angel error saved me thousands of dollars and gave me the opportunity to go to college in California.

After learning what manifesting truly was and how to do it, I have been able to actualize some pretty cool shit in the last three years, which has given me the nickname Manifesting Queen by my friends! I am often asked how do I manifest? There are many little things that I do, but the main thing I do is act as if I already am what I would like to become. I read this affirmation in Dr. Wayne Dyer's book, *The Power of Intention* and it permanently stuck with me. I have this affirmation alerted to me on my iPhone every day at 9:11 pm. I mentioned previously that 911 is one of the first angel numbers that popped up everywhere once I accepted my woo-woo ways. Wayne Dyer has been the biggest influence on me when it comes to manifesting the life I want. I have heard it over and over, "If you change your thoughts you can change your life." When I think about my connection with him, I sometimes doubt that connection. My ego tells me, Wayne wouldn't be bothered with someone who has only been following his teachings for only a few years. But, I know the connection is very real.

After reading *The Power of Intention*, I decided to set my intentions with everything I desired. I often call on Wayne to show me a sign that I am headed in the right direction. I learned that a huge part of manifesting was owning my strength and power in co-creating with the Universe. I made sure the Universe knew loud and clear what my dreams and intentions were.

This memoir that you are reading is one of my first manifestation projects, when I knew what manifesting was. As soon as I heard Doreen Virtue say at Angel Intuitive Class in October of 2015, "if you want to be a Hay House author, you have to build your social media platform," the prestige of being a Hay House author vibrated in my being. I knew that was what I wanted to be. I felt in my every heartbeat that my story would be perfect for Hay House, and finally, my voice would be heard, and maybe I could help myself while helping others by telling my truth. I got home, and the process began. I started writing in my journal every day, "I am a best-selling Hay House author of my spiritual memoir, *Came to Believe.*"

Building my social media platform turned into

owning my own business, coaching other spiritual entrepreneurs on how to create their platform with authenticity and integrity. Through manifesting *Came to Believe*, I also co-created myself a career I love in social media. I even published a guidebook course on it, too! Once I got back from my time with Doreen in 2015, I began to build my social media platform and write this memoir. I envisioned myself speaking at an "I Can Do It!" Hay House conference about my book. I didn't know all the details of how it would unfold, but I didn't let that keep me from getting started.

In January of 2016, I got an email from Hay House about a Writer's Course they offer in Maui with Doreen. I thought, "How perfect! Doreen was my first spiritual teacher, and I have so much gratitude for Hay House and how the books they publish have changed my life." I knew I had to go! I booked my flight and hotel right away for June of that year. All I needed to do was purchase my Hay House ticket for the workshop. I knew Hay House sometimes offered specials on these things, therefore, I was waiting to see if the ticket would go on sale. Then on January 27, 2016, I decided to put my super power of manifestation to work. I texted my friend Marina saying, "I am going to call into Doreen's Hay House radio show and see if she will gift me the Hay House Writer's Course." Marina and I were always encouraging of each other's dreams, but I sensed she thought I was rather crazy thinking I could do this. I think thousands of listeners try to call into Doreen's show, ten get though, and she takes about four calls a show. The odds were not in my favor.

I, however, thought it was a perfect idea! My first step in this manifestation masterpiece was setting my intention by telling my idea to Marina. Not only did I hope Doreen would gift me the writer's course, I really wanted guidance from Doreen about my memoir. It was pretty scary at the time, thinking about the secrets and shame I would reveal in it. Maybe I wasn't ready yet? Doreen had been very supportive of me on Instagram suggesting that she even read some of my articles for *Soul & Spirit Magazine*. Everyone who knows Doreen, knows how generous she is on her show and in-person engagements, I guess it wasn't so far-fetched, right? I had only tried to call into Doreen's show once before, on my 39th birthday March 4, 2015. I didn't get through. This time I was going to get through.

The next step I took was putting the Hay House Radio Show call-in number as a contact on my phone. I entered it as "Hay House Radio with four angel emoji's." Four has always been my lucky number, since my birthday landed on a four day. In angel numbers from www.angeltherapy.com, the number four means, "The angels are with you. They send you the number four to reassure you that they've heard your prayers and are helping you." Then I had typed "I will get picked with four more angel emoji's to follow." I then closed my eyes and called in my angels to help guide me in this manifestation and send whispers to Doreen to pick my phone line. I envisioned me getting through, I saw her picking my line, and I recited what our conversation would look like all in my third eye. My palms were sweaty, and I was nervous. I called in thirty minutes ahead a time and got through. YES!!! The Hay House employee asked, "Do you have a question for Anita?" At the time I had no idea who Anita Moorjani was, so I said, "Oh no, did I call too early? I am trying to get through for Doreen." The person politely told me to call back. I waited and called in five minutes before the show started and I got through on the ninth try!! Wooohooooo. When you get through, you listen to the radio show until someone from Hay House picks up the line. Finally, after twenty minutes someone picked up and asked me my name, where I was from, and what was my question. I said, "I am Tara, I am from Pasadena, my question is regarding writing a book, and having the confidence to do so." I was then put on hold and got to listen to the show while I waited. I just love Doreen and how kind and sweet she is. There were only about ten minutes left of the show, and I screamed at my iPhone, "Pick me, pick me, pick me!" My friend, Marina, was listening in and she told me that she too was saying, "Pick Tara, Pick Tara!" I was watching, "Hay House Radio, Angel emoji X's four, I Will Get Picked, Angel emoji X's four" scroll across my iPhone. I closed my eyes to tune in as I connected and pleaded with my angels for Doreen to pick my line.

I remember her asking, "Do we have time (for one more caller?)" I screamed at my phone, "Yesssssss, you have time!" Then Doreen said, "Yes, we have plenty of time!" She paused for a while going through the names and questions of the remaining callers. "This is a good one. Let's go to line 9 and speak to Ms. Tara, please." Oh My God! I got through!! I asked her about writing a book proposal and writing my book. She said, "I see you have already called on Archangel Gabriel, I see Gabriel with you. And I am hearing, "Keep on, keeping on and keep on the path that you are doing." Archangel Gabriel helps with writing books and other creative writing! I started to cry inside. I let her know the title of my book, *Came to Believe*. She said, "Wow,

149

powerful title, titles mean a lot." She then went on to tell me about book proposals and agents and how she was able to get published back in the 80's with Hay House. She gave me suggestions on how to find an agent. Then she says, "Let me ask Diane... Can I gift her the Writer's Course?" Diane said, "Yes!" I screamed out in excitement, jumped off my couch startling Chester. He began barking and running around in circles. She then said my advice to you is "Don't stop writing, write a page a day." She ended the call giving me "big sister hugs." I did it! I freaking did it! I manifested the Hay House Writer's Course!

I called my friend Marina after and rehashed the call! We were both amazed and excited! Marina told me, "You know it was the Hay House Online Writer's Course that she gifted you?"

Oh? I said, "Are you sure?" Marina was sure. I went back and listened, and she was right, it was the online course. I thought, "You know what? That was exactly what I was meant to get!" I couldn't stop smiling and in my head, I kept thinking, "Isn't it amazing? I manifested this! Although it wasn't exactly what I was picturing, my angels gave me exactly what I needed!" All I had to do was believe! Which is so fitting for my book title, *Came to Believe*.

This was why my reservations to Maui changed a few times landing me there on the one year anniversary of Dr. Wayne Dyer's death. And I took Doreen's advice and wrote almost every day. I have my iPhone alert me every morning with her prayer to Archangel Gabriel, "Dear Archangel Gabriel, thank you for giving me the courage, focus, and motivation to write. Thank you for helping me hear true Divine messages that I can express through word."

There are a lot of other things I do to help me manifest after I set my intention. My log-ins for almost everything has my book title within it in a secretly coded way. My passwords for websites and accounts are always encrypted in a way that manifests what I desire. I enter these passwords and logins multiple times a day, driving that energetic alignment home over and over again.

I mean really, I don't think the Universe and my Angels could ever be confused about what I want. I had a bracelet made with the *Came to Believe* stamped on the top and 11:11 stamped underneath. I also named my iPhone "I am a Hay House Best-Selling Author," and this is who Siri in a British Male accent refers me as. All of my alarms and affirmations are set to alert me at either 9:11, 11:11 or 1:11. My Wi-Fi network has some version of my book title in it. On

151

my daily gratitude list, I write, "Came to Believe." I use crystals to help me co-create with the Universe. I have become quite the crystal junkie over the last few years. I always have Larimar with me when I write. Judith Lukomski, who wrote *Crystal Therapy* with Doreen Virtue told me I should use Larimar to help me write from my heart. Larimar is said to enlighten and heal in a physical, emotional, mental and spiritual way. It stimulates the heart, throat, third eye and crown chakras facilitating inner wisdom and outer manifestation. It represents peace and clarity, radiating healing and love energy (from www.larimarket.com) Other excellent stones that I use all the time are Rose Quartz and Citrine. Both of these stones help with manifesting.

Another story of manifesting, that I am being guided to tell you, is my goal to become a Kundalini Yoga Teacher. I have been practicing Kundalini Yoga for 11 years now. I have been serious about my practice ever since I moved to Pasadena in 2013 and found a Kundalini Yoga studio that only taught Kundalini Yoga, The Awareness Center. I was very intentional about my practice and found teachers who moved me and really helped me connect to my Kundalini energy. In 2016, I decided I wanted to be a Kundalini Yoga Teacher. I wasn't sure where I would find the funds to do this, but I knew this was the path I needed to take. I wrote in my daily gratitude journal every day, "Kundalini Yoga." I put in my Angel Box, "Please help me to find the funds to pay for teacher training." I affirmed, "I am a Kundalini Yoga Teacher."

The next month my Yoga Teacher and the owner of The Awareness Center, Wahe Guru Kaur, approached me about doing social media for her studio. She had seen my work and really liked my approach. We agreed I would be their Marketing Manager at first on an energy exchange basis, where I could apply some of my energy exchange towards Kundalini Teacher Training! What? It happened again! I manifested the very thing I needed for the realization of my path to becoming a Yoga Teacher. Not only that, a few months after assisting her on an energy exchange basis, she hired me as a consultant. I was able to apply the money I made there, along with partial energy exchange credit, to pay for Kundalini Yoga Teacher Training in full without having to dip into my regular income or savings. I am now a certified Kundalini Yoga teacher and will be starting my Kundalini Yoga Teacher level two certifications. Sat Nam!

I have been able to manifest things other than financial assistance, like a creating a place to live in less than 48 hours when I needed to move at the drop of a hat! I was residing in a situation with a roommate that had become really unsafe for Chester. My roommate decided to bring home a dog from a shelter without discussing it with me ahead of time. She invited this dog into the house when I was not home, without having Chester and this new dog meet on leash and in neutral territory. I have no idea what really happened, but I got a phone call from my roommate telling me about the new dog and that Chester and this new dog got in a little fight, but Chester was fine. I came home, and Chester was hiding under my bed whimpering with over ten bites all over his back, neck, and face. I was having my first round of hammertoe surgeries in three days, and my gut was telling me that I needed to get out of there! The next day I drove up and down the streets calling my angels to help guide me to a safe place for myself and Chester. I found an apartment that day, on a Sunday, left a message with the rental company, looked at the apartment on Monday, filled out the application and moved in on Tuesday. My surgery was scheduled for Wednesday. I prayed to my angels as I filled out the application. I was nervous that I wouldn't get approved since I had recently filed for bankruptcy a year before. Everything fell into place perfectly, the apartment, my friends coming over to help me pack, the moving company being available and getting my new place settled before surgery.

Sometimes we can try so hard to force outcomes and mistake that for manifesting or strategically setting intentions. There is a balance of letting go and allowing the Divine to take the wheel. If it seems forced, then you are doing too much. All your angels need to hear from you is your clear intention statements, and they will get to work on what is best for you. Please do not get discouraged if something that you wanted to co-create with the Universe never reached the light. This has happened to me too. I will share in the last chapter an instance when one might say my manifesting went wrong, but it actually happened just as it should.

I am beyond grateful for my mad intention-setting skills. Setting clear intentions and communicating them to your angels is imperative. When you see your intentions transpire, be sure to show gratitude to the Universe and your Higher Power. When I am grateful for the miracles that come in my life, I create more manifesting miracles. Gratitude is one of the keys to successful actualization. It is the vehicle for high vibes of intention to kick into gear. So, what are you waiting for? What are you going to manifest today?

Chapter 12
I Am a Spirit Junkie

"Being an expression of our own healing has the power to heal others."
-Gabrielle Bernstein

I know the last chapter was all about manifesting the f' out of your life, but something else I was able to manifest was the miracle of attending Gabrielle Bernstein's Spirit Junkie Masterclass Level One and Level Two. Before getting into that, I want to tell you how I became a Spirit Junkie, part of a beautiful tribe of spirit seekers, light shiners and students of Gabrielle Bernstein, the author of *Spirit Junkie*, *May Cause Miracles* and *The Universe Has Your Back* to name a few. I had never heard of Gabby Bernstein until January 2016, when I took the Hay House Online Writer's Course. Her parts of the course I instantly connected with. There was something about her. She was authentic, vulnerable and very loving when she spoke with her audience. There was one audience member to whom she talked that made me want to look up this Gabby chick. The recording was from the New York Hay House Writer's Workshop, and she was taking a question from future Hay House author Danielle Shine. Danielle was asking a question about putting herself out there on social media and the game of getting likes and followers. It is so funny that this was her question, not knowing a few months later I would make a business out of social media. Gabby was so kind and sweet to Danielle. She asked her assistant to follow Danielle from her Instagram account and asked everyone in the room to do the same. I too followed Danielle at that time. Then, I followed Gabby. Literally in that order. Since then Danielle has been one of my biggest supporters on social media and in writing my book. Gabby's aura was evident even through a video; there was something magical about her. I Googled her and *Spirit Junkie* came up. I downloaded it on my iPad and began reading. Again, authenticity shined through this book, and I was extremely inspired and moved by her ability to be truthful and write with conviction. Everything she posted on her Instagram feed, resonated with me. It made me feel good about myself and confirmed I was on the right path.

Then one day she posted about an online workshop she was going to host called, "How Do You Do What You've Been Dreaming Of?" Thank goodness I took excellent notes to refer to for this chapter. The workshop was so huge that she broke the internet with it. A question she asked was, "Who does your story serve?" I am going to share what I wrote here because it is so telling of this memoir that you are currently reading.

I said, "I am here to do great work. I can serve anyone who wants to believe in something outside of themselves and anyone who wants to believe in manifesting their dreams. I can serve anyone who is a survivor and wants more from their life than what happened to them in their childhood, which is holding them back."

She went on to give us seven steps to be able to do what you have been dreaming of or at least seven steps are what I wrote down. Two of the pearls of wisdom that I gleaned from that talk were, "Bring an energy to your current job that supports your transition," and "Your wounds are your wisdom." Looking at my journal right now to write this chapter, I see that Gabby made my gratitude list on April 5th, 2016, for the first of many times. After this workshop, she announced her Spirit Junkie Masterclass. I immediately knew I wanted to go, and I would do whatever it took to get there. A few weeks later I saw she was giving away a scholarship for her Masterclass. I applied with a three-minute video, one of the first times I put myself in front of the camera, and just talked about myself. I won a partial scholarship to the Spirit Junkie Masterclass, booked my flight and stayed with a friend and her two children in a one bedroom condo in New Jersey. I do want to mention, if Doreen hadn't gifted me the Online Writer's Course, I would have been in Maui taking the in-person Writer's Workshop during the Spirit Junkie Masterclass, as they were both in June, very close to each other. At the time, I wouldn't have been able to afford jetting setting from Hawaii to New York. Everything happens for a reason.

I was super-nervous walking into the Spirit Junkie Masterclass on the first day. I am very much an introvert around strangers. One of the wonderful things that Gabby's team does before Masterclass is to invite everyone to an exclusive Facebook group of all those who have attended the class in the past. I had instant internet friends! It was nice to recognize some of the gorgeous faces whom I had seen in the group when I arrived. I didn't feel like a new kid in school who had no friends. I got there early enough to sit in the front row. It was so crazy when I saw Gabby come out on the stage and seeing her for the first time in person. Her energy is even more powerful, and her aura shines even brighter in real life than on the video I saw. I had a serious girl crush. I was nervous about her catching me staring at her that every time her eyes would find mine I would look down or look away. All I knew after that night was I wanted what she had. I wanted to shine bright, and I wanted to move people they way she did. Something she said that night was, "Even in my darkest moments, I am determined to see." Yes, I was, and I am, determined to see.

The next day, being the control freak I am, I got to the venue super early. It was nice to be there early, not only to get in the front row again (yes, I was one of those,) but I was able to connect with some beautiful angels in line like my girls, Kelsey Dalziel and Sarah Sapora, both of whom are doing big things! The second day was freaking powerful. Gabby's mission was to crack us open to get to the core of our limiting beliefs. She started the day off playing "Aad Guray Namey," which pulsated deep in my heart as the gorgeous voice of Jai Jagdeesh vibrated in the auditorium. *Aad Guray Namey* is a very powerful mantra used for protection, to gain clarity, and to receive guidance from one's Highest Self. This mantra creates a protective field of energy around the person chanting, attracting abundance to them and helping them live out their destiny. (from www.satnamfest.com) Tears rolled down my face. The tears would not stop. I was embarrassed by my tears, once I looked up and saw Gabby staring right at me. I wiped them quickly, as I always did when I

161

began to cry in front of others. After the song had ended Gabby went into a story about something that had happened to her in her childhood that shook me to the core. I knew exactly what she was talking about without her even having to say what it was specifically. It touched me and reminded me of what had happened to me. I couldn't even look at her at this point because I was afraid she would see the trauma in me, I was ashamed.

We then wrote down our old, limiting beliefs that were holding us back and formulated our freedom statement. As we were writing, she played Jai-Jaghdeesh's "Expand Through All Obstacles," which included the mantra, Aap Sahaaee Haoo. This mantra according to www.3ho.org, means the Creator has become my protector, the Truest of the True has taken care of me. I did this meditation for my 40 days, 31-minute meditation for Kundalini Yoga Teacher Training. When you chant this meditation, your hands are placed over your heart, left over right. As I listened to the words, tears streamed down my face, and I felt safe and protected around my old limiting belief. My freedom statement was, "Releasing fear gives me the freedom to let go of control. By doing so, I can breathe, be honest and vulnerable." And I did exactly that. The fastest way out of fear for me is to share about my shame. As the mantra was playing, Gabby said, "We have to get real, and we have to get honest about these wounds in order to allow them to move through us, to allow our bodies to get out of freeze mode. We have to allow ourselves to finally live and to finally be free."

I raised my hand later in the day as we were talking about different types of healing Kundalini meditations. After Gabby being vulnerable in the morning with her story and her seeing me cry uncontrollably, I felt a connection with her. I felt safe. She held space for many of us in the room to share our stories I knew I had to raise my hand. I was no longer concerned about the mascara smeared on my face. She saw it; I couldn't hide anymore. I was in it. Gabby called on me. I was shaking and nervous because what I was about to share I hadn't shared with very many people. I had just started to do recovery work around it with my therapist in March that year. As soon as I began to talk, she leaned in and was completely present, lovingly guiding me. I said, "I have a question about the meditations. I see there is a meditation for releasing childhood anger, but I need to get angry about what happened to me." She knew. She knew exactly what had happened to me. My therapist tells me for me to heal and relieve my anxiety, I need to get angry about the situation and my perpetrator. I shared about this

163

trauma and my inability to get angry at the person who hurt me with Gabby and my new loving spirit tribe like I have never shared it before. I talked about growing up in a home with the disease of alcoholism and the trauma I experienced in my home. I was terrified and filled with relief at the same time. I was energized and exhausted at my courage and strength to be vulnerable. When I first started my recovery in Alanon and when I would share with the group, I would leave before the meeting ended so I wouldn't have to talk to anyone after. This time, I faced my new friends and was received with love, validation, support, hugs, and resonation. For the first time, I didn't feel ashamed. Gabby listened intently to my story, offering me encouragement, love, and validation that I wasn't alone and that I was going to help many other survivors by sharing my story. I told her about this book and how I didn't want to include my trauma in the book and how my therapist told me I needed to. Gabby said, "You have a good therapist, you need to include this in your book." She also told me that even though I am still healing, I can still help others to heal by sharing my story.

Right after I shared a woman raised her hand and praised me for my vulnerability and sharing my story. She talked about how often the alcoholic or addict doesn't think about the wreckage and the pain they create with their loved one while in their disease. She admitted she was an alcoholic and congratulated me for doing the work in Alanon and taking care of myself. A few more women spoke up after me saying I inspired them to share their stories. On the third day, I sat more towards the back. The Spirit Junkie sister I sat next to revealed to me that she too endured the same thing I did and hadn't had the courage to talk to her therapist about it. She said I inspired her to share about her experience with her therapist when she got back home. So many women came up to me at the end of the day hugging me and thanking me. It was me that needed to thank them. They helped me to see that, even though I have had trauma after trauma, I can deeply and completely accept myself. The event ended with a book signing with Gabby. I whispered in her ear thanking her for creating the space for me to share what I did. She thanked me as if I helped her too. She hugged me tightly, or maybe it was me squeezing her. In that fleeting second, I knew we would be forever connected. I walked away from her, turned around and said, "I am going manifest the funds to go to Spirit Junkie Masterclass Level Two." She responded, "I know you will."

I sat on a delayed plane, waiting to head back to
Los Angeles, thinking about how the heck would I
get together the money to attend Level Two. I looked
at my phone and pulled up Facebook and saw that
Gabby was live on Facebook. Was this my sign that I
would go to Level Two? I asked my angels show me
another sign that it was meant to be and that the
abundance will flow to me. I said to my angels, "If
Gabby responds to my comment, then I will attend
Level Two." Gabby was talking about public
speaking. I remember writing in the comments
"always invite God in with you and focus on service."

I waited. I know this may seem nuts. I remember Gabby responding to comments after mine, so I thought, ok it isn't meant to be. Then she read my comment out loud and said, "There you go, Tara." I looked down at the clock, and it read 1:11, one of my angel numbers.

I worked hard manifesting the money for the Spirit Junkie Masterclass. It also helped that because my flight was delayed coming back from Level 1, I was given a $300 travel voucher. I bought my ticket to Spirit Junkie Masterclass Level Two a week after Level 1, putting it on a 0% interest credit card and trusting the Universe would provide me the money in time to pay it off before I would start to pay interest on it. Like clockwork, the Universe came through. I was on my way to Spirit Junkie Masterclass Level Two in November of 2016.

After Spirit Junkie Masterclass Level One I felt I had a rebirth. I walked with confidence. I felt validated. My shame lessened, I could be more vulnerable than I had ever been. My work with my therapist went deeper, as I allowed myself to feel those emotions I'd stuffed for so long. I stood in my authentic truth. I became grounded. I had support from this loving tribe. With all these new feelings, I was able to let go of old, limiting beliefs and pursue my life's purpose after I figured out what it was! That's another gift of the masterclass, after being true to me, I was able to learn what my purpose was. Who knew almost year after writing down who my story serves from Gabby's webinar, I would be writing this very chapter being of service with my story. I wanted to do whatever I could to support Gabby and spread her miracle messages. I felt a huge amount of gratitude for her that I almost felt I needed to repay her. I volunteered for all of her events that I could. I was truly happy to do it. It made me feel good!

When it was time for Level Two, much had changed in my life. I loved my Spirit Junkie sisters and felt thoroughly supported and loved by them. I was doing what moved me and felt deeply connected to my angels. Life was good. I lived in serenity and peace. I had just had reconstructive Hammer Toe surgery on both feet a month before Level Two, and I was still in pain and wearing two boots, but that wasn't going to stop me! It did not stop me. I called my Uber to pick me up about 2.5 hours before my red-eye flight out of LAX thinking that would be sufficient amount of time. Holy crap, it wasn't ... even though I was only ten minutes away from LAX. I was flying out to Massachusetts, Sunday after Thanksgiving. Traffic was a shit show. We sat in traffic for one hour on Sepulveda Boulevard, moving maybe one block. I freaking panicked!! I was so close, yet so far away with the snail's pace of gridlock traffic. 1.5 miles away exactly. I saw everyone ditching their families and Uber drivers to make the trek on foot to their gates. What the heck was I going to do? I was four weeks in with my recovery on my feet surgery. It was about 45 minutes until my aircraft was to take off and I was no closer than I was 20 minutes prior.

I asked the Uber guy, "What should I do?" He said, "You aren't going to make it unless you walk." I told him to pull over; there was no way I was going to miss my plane. I prayed to my angels to take over my feet and guide me to my gate. I jumped out of the Uber with my suitcase and joined the masses on foot, as my angels walked me there hand in hand. I made it to my gate minutes before boarding and was able to board first because of my sweet little feet! The flight crew got me some ice, and I was well on my way to Kripalu, Center for Yoga & Health in Stockbridge, Massachusetts, to Level Two!

I could write for hours about how transformative my experience was at Spirit Junkie Masterclass Level Two, but I will share just a few of my miracle moments. The first was seeing everyone and feeling their energy in person. I only knew a few of these light workers personally from Level One, the rest I became friends with through the worldwide web. Hugging everyone super tight and for longer than normal hugging times was necessary. I've been told my hugs are pretty magical, so I decided to go with it. When I hugged them, it felt like it wasn't our first hug. I can't explain it. These people will have my back in this lifetime and next. No joke, they probably had my back in my past lives too. My roommate Casey nursed my poor toes, gave me sound advice about my social media business, helped me with my transformational talk (my next miracle moment), and we stayed up laughing and talking all night long. The bond we built living in such small quarters, doing some intense work together, will never be forgotten. Then there is my soul sister Lissette to whom I grew extremely close after Level Two. First of all, her last name, LaRue, is pretty much the same as my last name, LaDue. LaRue and I had built a bond at Level One at first because of our last names. It grew to be so much more. We talk about everything together. We feel safe sharing our deepest secrets, and we encourage and support each other. We text daily and talk weekly. I can't image my life without my girl LaRue.

There were countless miracle moments, but I will

share just one more. I was able to give my transformation talk in front of Gabby and my fellows. Giving my transformational speech in a safe space of beautiful beings and receiving feedback from Gabby Bernstein was invaluable. This is seriously priceless for a multitude of reasons. In the talk, I shared about some milestones in my healing from the same childhood trauma I lightly mentioned at Level One, that I haven't had the courage to talk about (only write about) until then. There is something about speaking your story and hearing your voice that makes stuff get real, super-fast. I am so grateful Casey recorded the talk for me. Casey even told me my story was "Ted Talk worthy!" The feedback from Gabby came from a place of kindness, compassion and was very encouraging. She said, "The story is extremely important, and we need it, Tara." Gabby taught me about what a core message was, which helped me to come up with the tagline for this book, "A Journey of Trust, Faith, and Perseverance." She also taught me what it feels like and what it means to speak and teach with conviction. There is not one person that I have seen stand beautifully in their imperfections more than she does.

It is not hard for me to express the amount of love and gratitude I have for Gabby and the Spirit Junkie community. Gabby feels like an older sister to me, even though I am older than she is. She makes an effort to stay connected with me and inspires me to continue on my healing journey. This tribe is my family. I am closer and feel more love from them than I do from those who have known me my entire life. Being a Spirit Junkie is a gift. I would never take it for granted. I am so proud of the work I have done and my willingness to expose my shameful, dark secrets. I am beyond grateful to call myself a Spirit Junkie.

Chapter 13
We Are Only as Sick as Our Secrets

"And the truth shall set you free."
-John 8:32

Dear Tara,

I can't even imagine what you must have felt like, a little girl being violated the way that you were, even though I was there. When I think of this happening to a young child I love so much in my life, it makes me sick inside. To see her eyes and face as it was going on, makes me cry. When I look at your picture as a little girl, I see such innocence, purity, and love. How could you defend yourself and speak up for yourself when you were so small? You must have been terrified. I feel much sadness and compassion for you. You were trapped and couldn't protect yourself. You were powerless. You should have been protected. This should have never happened to you, over and over again. I know you were just trying to be a good little girl by staying out of the way and being invisible amongst the chaos. It was better for you to stay quiet and small, rather than cause more stress and drama to your mom by being honest and telling your truth. But, you matter, too. You, especially matter because you were so young and trusting. Your safety matters. Your feelings matter. I want you to know that you didn't cause this incest to happen, it wasn't your fault. Please forgive yourself and no longer allow the abuse to paralyze your ability to connect with men and women. You are a sweet and innocent child of God and it is okay for you to trust others. Release this pain that has been binding you. It no longer serves you. Let go of the shame and be free. Enjoy connection and relationships, particularly with men. You are worth it.

With love,

Tara

My therapist advised me to write this letter to my five-year-old self as part of an exercise from the book *Courage to Heal, A Guide for Women Survivors of Sexual Abuse.* I started to see a therapist just before my 40th birthday in March of 2016. I had tried therapy in the past to heal this trauma from my youth, but I wasn't ready. I am ready now. I am a survivor of incest. My eldest adopted brother molested me when we were younger. This has been my secret until now. Neither of my parents knew what was happening during this time. It was no one's fault. I had mentioned it very lightly in Alanon

174

meetings, but only labeling it as molestation or childhood sexual abuse and never going into detail. The word incest was so shameful to me. Shame exists in an environment of secrecy. It terrified me to tell anyone what had happened to me. I stayed in silence until I was 24 years old. The individual I told for the first time didn't receive it very well. They were not in the position to hear me. They almost questioned my truth around it, and then denied that it was "that bad," after I explained a specific incident. I never really talked about it again, until recently. I pushed it way deep inside my soul, sealed it shut and thought I could forget about it. I couldn't. It affected me deeply and had power over me. I desperately wanted my power back. My power is mine and no one else's. If I choose to share my power with someone, it should be by my own free will not by force. The person I told originally recently revisited the topic with me. The conversation was loving, beautiful and so healing. I was validated and supported and I knew how transformational this validation was going to be for my healing journey.

Intimacy = into me I see. I had no idea what intimacy was. Some confuse intimacy with sex and are unaware of an intimate connection with another or self that did not include any physical interaction.

175

I learned what intimacy was through my Alanon program. I later realized that I didn't have intimacy with anyone, including myself. This trauma from my childhood plagued me when it came to trusting men and even women. For me to walk into a therapist office on my knees to ask for help to heal from the incest was such a huge step towards my freedom and love towards myself. My angels brought me to my knees with this. They gave me sweet nudges and encouragement. All of my spiritual endeavors and work in Alanon had brought me to this point. In the last chapter, I told the story of how I came clean with my trauma to a room of 300 Spirit Junkies and how liberating that felt! For me to feel safe enough to reveal that hidden shadow of myself took three months of therapy, my angels, a strong desire to heal and being in the safest place at the perfect time with the most loving souls. By shedding a layer of shame with my story that day, it propelled me even further on the healing path.

I was pretty strategic about the way I picked my therapist. Strategic or controlling? At this point it doesn't matter. I knew I wanted a female therapist because of the nature of the trauma. However, that didn't stop me from picking a male gynecologist. Ultimately, I picked my therapist because of her picture. She had a kind and warm smile and I felt she would understand me. There was a glow around her face, almost as if she was one of my angels urging me to pick her. She has bright blue eyes and dimples. After I decided on this therapist, I used Doreen Virtue and Radleigh Valentines Angel Answers Oracle Cards and asked, "Is she the one? Will she be able to help me?" The card I pulled? "Yes!"

It was a big deal to tell my story to someone else and know that I would have to come back the next week and face what I said and talk some more about it. I felt I could get from her what I so desperately needed from the first person I told. When I shared about it at Alanon meetings, I would leave early. I didn't have the courage to face people that I just shared this shameful secret with. I wouldn't go back to that meeting for a few weeks in hopes they would forget what I had admitted or forget who I was all together. Going to therapy is a commitment. I was ready to be committed to this therapist, which was the first round of intimacy with another person I experienced outside of my sponsors in Alanon. I was proud of myself for going to my first session with my therapist, and most importantly, that I am continuing this act of self-care and self-love today. I have even started EMDR, Eye Movement Desensitization and Reprocessing with this therapist adding another layer of healing.

I started to feel a weight being lifted off me. I could breathe smoothly and let go. My angels, my therapist, 300 Spirit Junkies, and my Alanon sisters all had my back through this process. I was no longer alone in this. People loved me no matter what. I began to write more and more about my trauma. This helped me create intimacy with myself. Something about writing my feelings out on paper was a release and a connection to my inner spirit that I hadn't felt before. *Courage to Heal, A Guide for Women Survivors of Sexual Abuse* has a lot of beautiful tear-inviting writing exercises like the one at the start of this chapter. Something about crying for me cleaned the slate of shame and sadness. Calmness would overcome me. One of the writing suggestions from this book is to start off writing, "I remember when...." and begin to free write without stopping. So, I wrote what I was feeling, smelling and hearing at the time the abuse happened. The assignment asks that when you lift your head up to think then you put your head back down and start again with, "I remember when..." I did precisely that. Tears flowed from my eyes. Weird stuff came up in the writing that I had no idea would. Memories unfolded that frightened me. I became confused. I sat with this confusion and didn't know what to do with it. I started to have nightmares of images of the abuse and different ages of when it happened. I wouldn't see my therapist for another week to digest all this new information.

Can you imagine having images of a childhood abuse and seeing things happen to you at ages when you weren't aware the abuse happened? I thought my mind was playing tricks on me. I was completely freaked out. I believed the incest happened only when I was around five to nine years old. I am not sure what this meant and how it changed things if it even did. So much fear and turmoil was coming up for me, that I asked myself, "Why did I get into this? It would have been easier to not feel this pain." My ego entered again trying to suck me back to where I was before by convincing me I was too old to heal.

Thank goodness for my angels sending me compassionate signs of their support, reminding me that I wasn't alone, muting my ego and returning me to self-love. I talked to my angels about my fear. Sometimes I have a conversation with them in my head, out loud or on paper. It doesn't really matter because your angels always hear you when you reach out to them and even when you aren't consciously doing it. They always listen to the thoughts in your head. At this time, I felt a warm embrace. My angels whispered to me that I was strong and to use my strength to feel these emotions. I had been told that my whole life, "You are so strong." I used to associate strength with not feeling any emotion and acting as if nothing happened as I always did. Just brush it off, I was fine. On this day, my angels gave me the true definition of strength: to honor my feelings and release them to my Higher Power. I continue to sort out my memories and visions around my abuse. My therapist asked me, "Do you think it changes things knowing the additional memories you uncovered in the writing and dreams?"

It only triggered more sadness and a bit more anger thinking about it. These new memories explained a few things for me. But, I know the work around the recovery all boils down to the same thing, I was still ready to heal and I needed to keep feeling my feelings in order to heal. I answered her, "I am not sure if that is like saying, 'it shouldn't affect you as much because it only happened once or I am worse off than you because I endured sexual abuse for this many years as opposed to less.'" She agreed with me. It only needs to happen one time for a person to feel powerless, alone, violated and shamed. I needn't diminish what I went through no matter how many times it happened, when, and to what extent.

I started Tapping, EFT, (Emotional Freedom
Technique) to help me when I feel anxiety around
my healing journey. I also use EFT with any
thoughts or behaviors that are not serving me. I also
just recently started tapping on my sugar addiction.
It was something I heard about on the plane to Spirit
Junkie Master Class while listing to Gabby
Bernstein's *Miracles Now* audio book. At first, I was a
worried that some would think I was a weirdo
tapping my face and under my arm, but I tried it on
the plane anyway. When I was doing it then I went
right into the tapping without stating my MPI, "Most
pressing issue," but the physical act of tapping
calmed me anyway. Maybe my angels stepped up for
me with my MPI! I wouldn't doubt it. Then, when I
was at Spirit Junkie Masterclass, Gabby did EFT on a
few students and I played along with their sessions.
She even mentioned that she thought it would help
me with my childhood trauma along with EMDR
when I asked my question. Doing it with those few
people allowed me to surrender to the feelings I was
having around my fears in class that morning. I'm a
new to EFT, but I did order Nick Ortner's *The
Tapping Solution*, which I started to read while flying
to Maui in August 2016.

On the plane to Maui I came up with my MPI statement. I said, "Even though the shame of the incest has disabled me in love, I completely love and respect myself." I was feeling about an eight on the "SUDS" scale (Subjective Units of Distress Scale) because of sitting between two men on this flight, which brought me anxiety. The goal was to get it down to a two or three. If I was super ambitious, then I would tap until I got to a zero. I said my MPI statement three times to myself on the plane. I am not sure what it is about being on a plane and EFT for me, but I went with it:

- I tapped on my karate chop point while flying to one of the most beautiful places on the planet, repeating, "Even though the shame of the incest has disabled me in love, I completely love and respect myself."

- Then I said, "I hate that my shame has made me so afraid of intimacy," as I tapped above my eyebrow five times.

- Then I moved to the side of my eyebrow and while tapping said, "I hate that this shame has made me so afraid of intimacy. I am so embarrassed about it." I repeated my first statement because it was so significant for me to

182

admit and adding the embarrassment was a hard truth I kept to myself.

- I moved to under my eye and tapped, "Even though I am so afraid of intimacy I completely love and accept myself."

- Then I moved to under my nose and began tapping, "This abuse has had power over me and the ability to trust others."

- I moved to my chin and while tapping said, "Even though I have a hard time trusting others, specifically men, I completely love and respect myself."

- Then I moved to tapping on my collarbone and said, "It is time for me to trust people. It is okay for me to trust people. I do not need to be embarrassed or ashamed."

- Next, I said, "I am ready to release this shame and heal these old limiting beliefs that no longer serve me," as I was tapping under my arm.

- Finally, I was tapping on my head and repeated the last statement. "I am ready to release this shame and heal these old limiting beliefs that no longer serve me."

I was able to get myself from an eight to a two, after two rounds going through the EFT process. I now use EFT as part of my spiritual practice. Spirit really led me to this technique. I am grateful I heard about this through the *Miracles Now* book. In fact, on my plane ride back from Maui, a Mom and her daughter noticed I was reading Nick Ortner's book. They asked me what I thought of it. I told them I had just started to read it, but had actually been tapping for a few months now. I let them know that it had changed my life and how I deal with anxiety and stress. The Mom had heard of the book because she subscribed to Nick Ortner's email list. She said she kept forwarding the emails to her daughter hoping she would try it. The daughter asked me, "Has it really helped you?" I answered, "Completely." The Mom then said, "See, it's a sign."

I have found that forgiveness is one of the biggest parts of healing from any abuse. This includes forgiveness of yourself, along with the individual who harmed you. *A Course in Miracles* says, "Do you want a quietness that cannot be disturbed, a gentleness that never can hurt, a deep abiding comfort, and a rest so perfect it can never be upset? ... All this forgiveness offers you, and more." I forgave the person who did this to me. I have a lot of compassion towards them. I know they were hurting too, and by no means does this excuse the behavior, but it does allow me to send them love and light and hope they can get better too. I am one of the lucky ones. Although my healing journey has a long way to go, I am sure there's a book to be written down the road, I no longer sit silently in my shame.

I wanted to include a forgiveness letter that I wrote to my perpetrator as part of an assignment in Gabby Bernstein's *May Cause Miracles*:

Dear person, who hurt me,

You should have been someone who was safe. I would have never expected something like this to happen from someone I knew. I was young, trusting and open to receive love. I am sure you were too. I am trying to be angry at you. I want to be angry. I need to get angry. How could you take advantage of me? I haven't been able to get angry because of the compassion I have for you. I was fulfilling a need for you and wanted to make you happy because you protected me. I was confused. I couldn't stand up for myself. Nothing was okay about this. It was not okay for you to violate me and take advantage of me. I was scared and voiceless. I hate that you did this to me because it has affected me deeply, when it comes to relationships with men. I do not trust men. I have had a hard time being intimate with men because of fear and shame. Here I am 40 years old and I haven't experienced a loving relationship with a man and I am embarrassed about it. As a young girl and teenager, I was trapped by your power. I recognize now that you were hurting too, which doesn't excuse your actions, but it helps me to forgive you and release this shame. This shame is hurting me and damaging me. I no longer need it. I forgive you, and I forgive myself. I am ready to move past this and enjoy intimacy. I am ready to learn to trust men. I am not afraid of men. Men do not scare me. My hope for you is that you find help too.

Now, when I get scared or confused during this healing process, I turn to my journal and write my thoughts without censor. I share these with my therapist who makes me feel safe and protected or I call one of my spiritual sisters. Each week it gets better and better. I even started an online private serenity circle, so people can share their stories in a safe place. The more I share my story, the more I see how much I empower others to share theirs. This makes me feel beautiful inside. I also remind myself to be gentle on my healing process. There is no right way or exact timeframe to recover from childhood incest. I tap and I tap some more. I remember forgiveness and compassion, not just for the abuser, but for myself. I am so grateful for my therapist, my Spirit Junkie sisters, close friends and my angels to whom I can talk openly about my incest, so I no longer have to suffer and be terrified of love and intimacy. When I began to speak the truth freely about my abuse, the sense of shame dissipated. Speak the truth and the truth shall set you free. You are only as sick as your secrets.

Chapter 14
Came to Believe

"She believed she could, so she did."
-R.S. Grey

I did it! I am so freaking proud of this Spiritual Memoir. It had been my dream since my twenties to publish my story. Here I am typing out this last chapter, and I feel wonderful, accomplished and blessed. You would think after reading up until now that *Came to Believe* did get published by Hay House. I mean this book is pretty much a walking advertisement for all things Hay House. I thought I did everything right. I am a manifesting queen after all. Before you go looking at the back cover to see Hay House's name there, I did not win the Hay House Writers Contest and my book, at least until today, did not get published by Hay House. This just means that the Universe has other plans for my story and how it reaches the masses.

You might be thinking, "What went wrong?" Trust me; I asked myself that question for a few days after I found out the news. My ego got the best of me and made me feel like my story wasn't good enough, I didn't have enough followers on social media, or they just thought my grammar completely sucked. (I am not the best at grammar, so that last part could be true.) Everyone told me they thought I was going to win! Some even said they couldn't see it any other way! When I did my 2017 annual angel card reading in January of 2017 some interesting signs were given to me. In February when the Hay House contest was announced the card "Time to move on," came up and in March I pulled "Stay Optimistic." I had a weird feeling I wasn't going to win. When Hay House made the announcement, I put the book aside for two months. I honestly didn't know what to do or how to move forward. I thought this last chapter was going be all about how I did it! I fucking manifested being a Hay House author! But, that's not what this chapter is about now.

The truth is, nothing went wrong that day they made the announcement, and my name wasn't listed as the winner. Something went right. So many things went right. I may not have won that $10,000 contract and be able to say I am a Best-Selling Hay House author and stand beside those who taught me and inspired me; but, many other gifts and miracles came out of the process of writing my Spiritual Memoir. There is a saying in Alanon, "Rejection is God's protection." Not that I was rejected, but my Higher Power certainly had other things in mind for this memoir.

The first miracle from writing this book was telling my truth for the first time. I was completely vulnerable in this book, even at times when it hurt badly, and I was scared shitless of what my family and readers might think of me. One's authenticity is so vital today. If you can't shine in your radiance, if your Aura can't glow the way it wants to, what is the point of this life? I am telling you, finally after 40 years, I am exactly who I am meant to be, and I can say this with conviction. It is so liberating to unleash the darkness and to shine like the brightest crystal there is.

Another gift through this process was being introduced to many evolved souls and spiritual teachers in the Hay House Writer's Course. Before I took that course, I only knew Doreen Virtue, and I had read one Dr. Wayne Dyer and one Caroline Myss book. Getting a different perspective from teachers like Marianne Williamson, Kris Carr, Kyle Gray and Gabrielle Bernstein was such an opportunity! I read tons of self-help books to get an idea of how I would write my book, which enlightened me in ways I'd never imagined. I learned about manifesting the *f"* out of my life from the late Dr. Wayne Dyer. He showed me that my thoughts carry weight, and I couldn't go around with a *piss poor* attitude in my victim body if I wanted to materialize the life I longed for. Doreen Virtue made me feel, "Normal" being woo-woo embracing my love of angels. She gave me the confidence that I can feel the angels around me and trust their guidance. Caroline Myss taught me to stop feeling sorry for myself because I didn't have the white picket fence with two parents and everything at my disposal. Finding Gabby Bernstein and my Spirit Junkie tribe took my world to a higher level. With Gabby, I finally found the teacher that spoke my language, wasn't afraid to be imperfect and genuinely cared about my healing journey. All of these incredible superstars helped me to see my true potential. They showed me what worked for them and helped me to apply the same principles to my life.

Came to Believe is a journey of trust, faith, and perseverance. I am simply a woman from Phoenix, Arizona, who had some unfortunate things happen in her childhood. Sadly, I am sure there are many who share similar stories but haven't had the courage to come forward. I am hoping by writing this book, and sharing all the beautiful miracles I experienced, I might help others to speak up. I want to show people that by me trusting in a power outside of myself and knowing that my life happened exactly the way it was supposed to, all the darkness, and most importantly all the light, I was able to let go and let God. Having faith that I was Divinely protected allowed me to do the healing work. Maybe I might help others to move forward and come to forgiveness too. Maybe my story will give them strength to unbind the hostage that has been living inside their body and set it free.

There is so much more to be revealed in my spiritual journey. I often recite the mantra by Yogi Bhajan, the Master of Kundalini Yoga, "Keep up, and you will be kept up." Anything can happen, and I am ready. I have so many tools to guide me on my path of healing. I have Alanon, my sponsor, tapping, EMDR, my therapist, *A Course of Miracles*, my angels and Higher Power, Kundalini Yoga, all of my Spiritual teachers and my Spirit Junkie family. I am fully supported. I am still early in my recovery from childhood incest. But I will say that I can speak and type the word *incest* with much more ease and a lot less shame than when I first started writing this book in January 2016. I even went back in the edits and changed the words, "childhood trauma" and "sexual abuse," to "incest." I already have the outline and title of my second book which will be about my journey healing from incest through the 12 steps, therapy, EFT, EMDR and Kundalini Yoga.

My mom and my relationship continues to be

solid and balanced. I have found the compassion for her that had been missing before working my steps in Alanon. I love her completely. She understands me. She accepts my woo-woo side and, although she can't voice exactly how she feels about my early years and what happened, she is now at a place where she is proud of the achievements I have had in therapy and Alanon.

Just recently a spiritual teacher of mine honored me in a video about women turning their pain into progress. When this teacher made her video, I don't think she had an idea of the impact that it would have on my mother and my relationship. I shared the video on my personal Facebook page, and my mom saw it. Lord bless my mom, she has no clue how to operate Facebook, but she figured out how to share this video to her newsfeed and comment that she was proud of me. Hearing a New York Times #1 Best Selling Author honor the work I have done around my childhood trauma made it real for my mom. When I saw that post from my mom, I burst into tears. We never talked about her re-posting that, but we didn't have to. I was able to see this teacher after the video and thank her for what she did. I told her what my mom had done and how our relationship has been since, and she said with tears welling in her eyes, "When they asked me to honor someone, there was no doubt in my mind that it would be you."

I always believed I could do anything I set my mind to. I knew there was something about me that the world needed to hear, or in this case read. I believed I was meant to share my story. I believed I could, so I did.

"It's time to leave the past behind. Just let go, let's unwind. Ease your body, rest your mind. Go within, see what we find."

-Gurunam Singh

Acknowledgements

"If you just feel happy for what you have, have an attitude of gratitude, and be grateful, then it will come true, you will be great and you will be full."
-Yogi Bhajan

Mom, I love you. Thank you for being my best friend. Gabby Bernstein, thank you for your authenticity, your love, and for being my teacher. You are a gift to me. My Spirit Junkie family, you held me at a time I needed to be heard, and your continuous support is cherished. My longtime friends, Mala, Cristin, and Mythanh, thank you for always taking my call. Chester, I am obsessed with you.

My Kundalini Yoga Studio, The Awareness Center for keeping my chakras happy. My editor, Chelle Thompson, I learned more about grammar in this process than my whole life. My Angels, I am grateful you show me the way, daily.

In major gratitude for the guidance from NE Donavan, Wahe Guru Kaur and my therapist.

To you, my readers, of my first freaking book! Thank you, for hearing me and for believing in me. Thank you for showing others that it's possible to self-publish a book and that people will be moved by your message. Dream bigger, you can do it.

Came to Believe Book Cover Story

This book cover is so magical that I felt strongly that it needed its own special page in the book to explain its significance.

The cover shows the exact location of where I broke my ankle at Broad Beach in Malibu, California on September 2, 2014. The picture was taken by Dawnley B. Photography three years after my spiritual awakening. I had visited this location a few times after I broke my ankle, but on this day it was extra heavenly. A full circle moment. My dream of publishing a book was about to come true. I manifested this with my angels' help.

I am wearing white on the cover. In the past, I hated to wear white. I never owned white clothing before taking Kundalini Yoga Teacher Training. Yogi Bhajan taught us that wearing all white clothing expands our auric radiance by at least one foot. That is a good thing. A deep-seated aura gives us a powerful and solid identity and projection, and negative influences are automatically filtered. (from 3ho.org) I hope you can feel my aura in this photo.

The singing bowl. I bought this singing bowl as a

present to myself for graduating from Spirit Junkie Masterclass Level 2 at the Kripalu gift shop. I was worried some might think the cover was too spiritual having the mystical bowl in my lap and they wouldn't purchase *Came to Believe*. But then I reminded myself that this is my authentic self. This is me. Every part of me. Take it and love it, for I am unapologetically spiritual.

Sat Nam.

Book Cover designed by Kathleen Kranack, my Spirit Junkie sister. www.kranack.com

About the Author

Tara LaDue is the author of *Came to Believe, A Journey of Trust, Faith and Perseverance.* She is a Social Media Coach for Spiritual Entrepreneurs all over the world. She has written a Social Media Guidebook with all her own tips and tricks used to grow her following. Tara is a Certified Kundalini Yoga Teacher. She also is a Certified Angel Card Reader™ and Angel Intuitive®. Tara has taken Gabrielle Bernstein's Spirit Junkie Masterclass Level 1 and 2. She is the proud mommy of her fur-angel, Chester Harold LaDue.

For more information in Tara

For more information on Tara's work, visit www.taraladue.com. For daily inspiration and all around high vibes please join her on Social Media:

 @taraladue

 @serenityoftheangels

 @taraladue

Resources

*"Our deepest fear is not that we are inadequate.
Our deepest fear is that we are powerful beyond
measure. It is our light, not our darkness
that most frightens us."*
-Marianne Williamson

Alanon
www.al-anon.org

EFT, Emotional Freedom Technique
www.thetappingsolution.com

EMDR, Eye Movement Desensitization and
Reprocessing
www.emdr.com

Books:
A Course in Miracles
www.acim.org

Angels of Abundance
Doreen Virtue

Angels 101
Doreen Virtue

Anatomy of the Spirit
Caroline Myss

A Woman's Worth
Marianne Williamson

Chakras for Beginners
David Pond

Crystal Therapy
Doreen Virtue and Judith Lukomski

Daily Guidance from your Angels Oracle Cards
Doreen Virtue

Defy Gravity
Caroline Myss

Inspiration
Wayne Dyer

Many Lives, Many Masters
Brian Weiss

May Cause Miracles
Gabrielle Bernstein

Miracles Now
Gabrielle Bernstein

Pathways to Recovery
Alanon Conference Approved Literature

Power of Intention
Wayne Dyer

Spirit Junkie
Gabrielle Bernstein

Courage to Heal, A Guide for Women Survivors of Sexual Abuse
Ellen Bass and Laura Davis

The Tapping Solution
Nick Ortner

The Universe Has Your Back
Gabrielle Bernstein

64846697R00117

Made in the USA
San Bernardino, CA
26 December 2017